Edited by Dr. David T. Blomquist

INTRODUCTION

As far as we know, life on Earth has had a complicated and still not well-defined beginning.

However, what most enchants is the amazing evolution that it has had, with the realization of the wonderful and infinite forms that we can observe and with which humans (an integral part of these forms) interact.

We know that the biological processes of this extraordinary phenomenon, once activated, take place with incessant self-reproductive mechanisms.

These processes have meant that on the stage of life on Earth, among many others, a very particular structure assumed a fundamental role. Its intrinsic functioning is at the limits of the same biological rules that have determined its great level of sophistication and complexity, this is the "human brain".

The idea behind the considerations set out in this essay is to offer a different perspective on the aspects of human life and how it is managed by all the functioning brains.

All this in the attempt, probably utopian, to correct a characteristic of humans: the scarce propensity to interpret behaviors in their naturalistic essence, on the contrary attributing to them a more transcendent meaning.

Below are some images of human behavior, some simple and other more sophisticated. All however quite common or known.

For each of them let's try to ask ourselves, with a certain level of scientific curiosity and avoiding ethical-moral prejudices, why it is they...

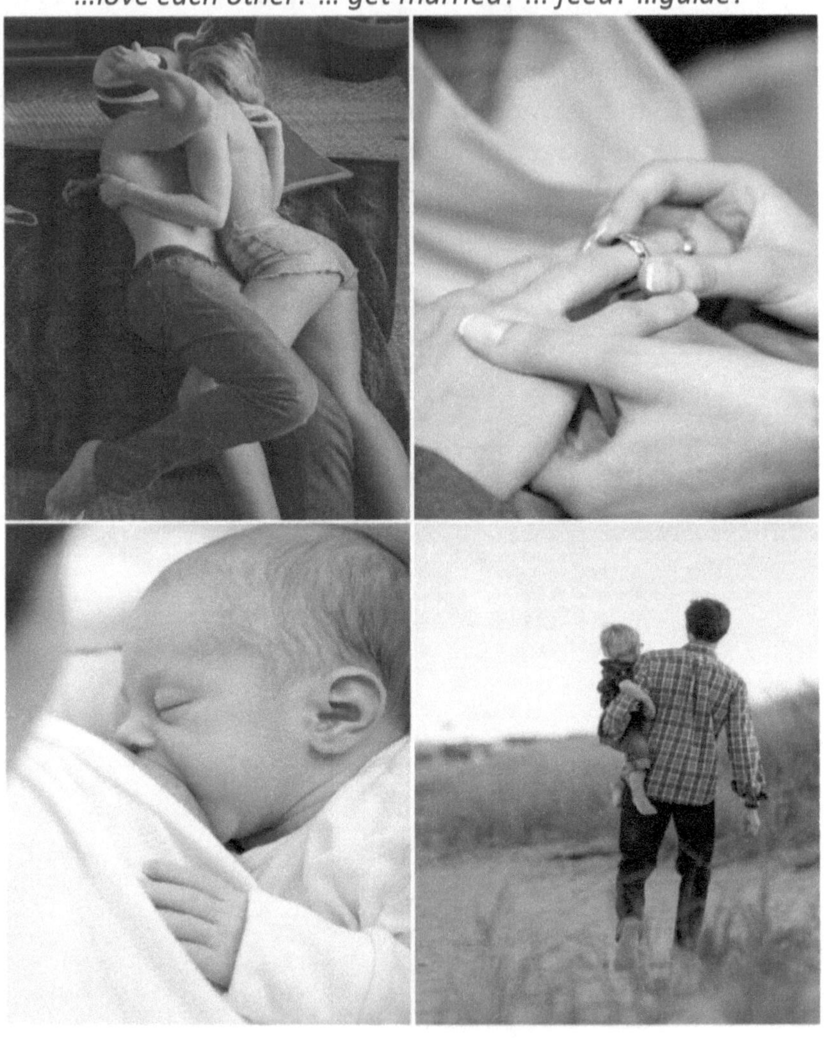

...risk? ... research? ... pray? ...teach? ...compete? ...take drugs?

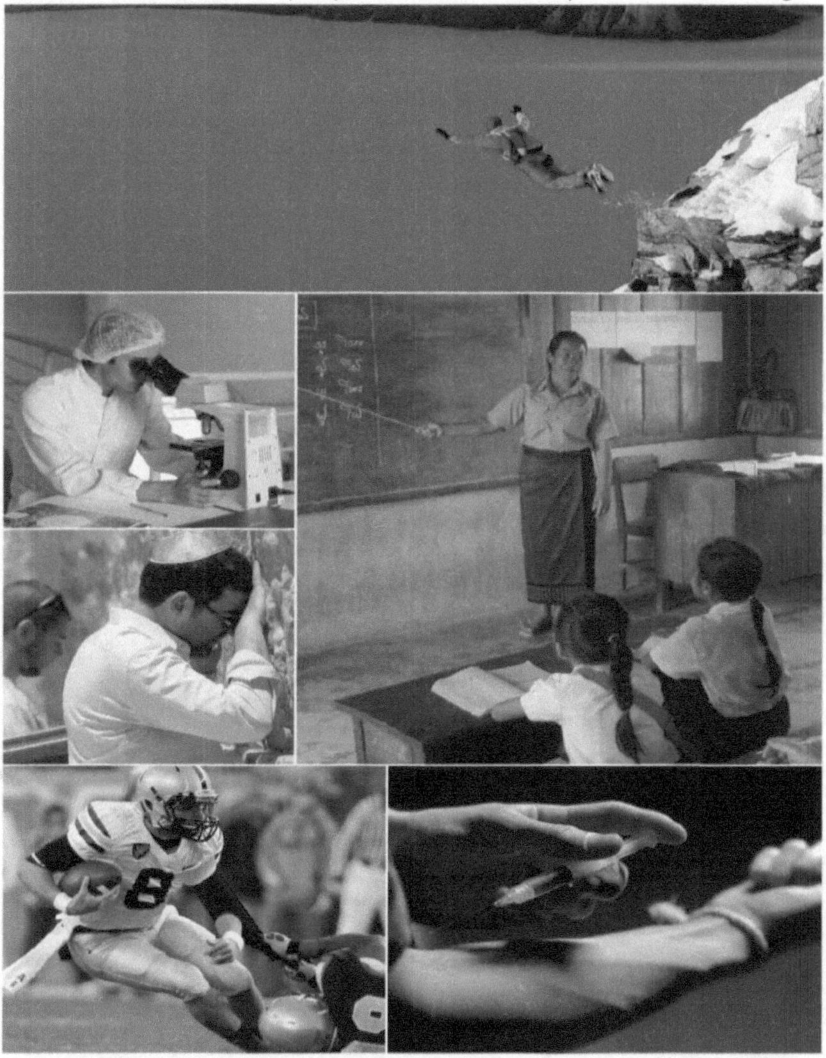

7

Obviously, those highlighted above are just some of the numerous human behaviors that could lead to reflections on their meaning in a psycho-socio-anthropological key.

They, like many others, offer us the opportunity to ask ourselves:

- "Why do humans do these things, in these ways?"

- "Are there other living species engaged in similar activities?"

For this last question, the answer is simple, and clearly, it is negative.

Let us look, for example, at chimpanzees, the living being that is closest to humans on the evolutionary ladder.

While chimpanzees share 98.77% of their DNA with our species, this "hominid" is far from being able to interpret, even approximately, specific features of the above-mentioned behaviors.

In some cases, they can learn simple, improvised behaviors, thanks to special training techniques (designed by humans) such as those used in circuses.

Despite these cases, however sophisticated they may seem, they will never be an integral part of complex behavioral strategies, aimed at achieving precise objectives.

The same applies to other domesticated animal species (dogs, dolphins, horses, elephants).

Coming to the first question, instead, the answer is very complex and articulated.

Let's start by saying that every single action performed by any living being has a specific purpose and it is triggered and supported by specific motivational mechanisms.

The natural site in which all these processes take place is the brain, the magnificent structure of command and control.
Therefore, even if we do not usually spend much time thinking about why we perform certain actions, even if complex, risky, expensive, extravagant, these are always the products of the admirable and coordinated activation of precise neuronal circuits located in the brain.
At this point, however, some clarification is needed.
The examples of behaviors reported above, as evident, are more represented in human communities classified as "western civilizations" or in any case industrialized. But behavior aimed at the same purposes, even if in less expensive and sophisticated forms are also present in less modernized human communities.
 The common denominators for all functioning brains are:
- program what to do
- implement what they have decided to do
- evaluate the result of what has been done.
All with varying levels of complexity.

Adoration, entertainment, motherhood, customs and discipline
in technologically not advanced civilizations

10

Based on these preliminary considerations, we can move forward with a different attitude in the examination of human behaviors and the incredible paradoxes of which we are protagonists in everyday life.

Why this book? There are several reasons.

First, to confirm, if ever it were needed, that man is really an "animal" with exceptional characteristics. The first among the primates.

Today the human-animal[1], thanks to the sophistication of its brain, is able to amaze itself with ingenious inventions, to reflect on the meaning of life with fascinating explanations, to investigate retrospectively about its origins up to establish and describe in a very detailed manner the evolutionary continuity and the history that interested it.

Thanks to its intelligence it has succeeded in identifying the smallest components of the material, almost reaching pure energy, taming and using it.

But alongside these exceptional functional properties, several highly irrational functioning mechanisms coexist, which the human-animal (or rather its "brain") recognizes but fails to regulate in a virtuous manner.

Hence the enormous difficulty in achieving the most natural biological condition that exists: homeostasis, a dynamic stability between internal and external biochemical balances to which all systems spontaneously tend. This dynamic state of

---

[1] The term "human-animal" is not used in a reductive way but merely in an anthropological sense. The attempt is to carry out, indirectly, a sort of critical comparison between the human being, holder of extraordinary abilities, and the remaining part of the animal kingdom, and therefore establish that the positive characteristics and potentials achieved during his evolution are still to be exploited.

equilibrium is the condition of optimal functioning. Conversely, the result of an imbalance has a significant impact on individual survival and on that of the entire terrestrial ecosystem.
Come to think of it, seriously and with a scientific approach, all this seems paradoxical!

Some spontaneous reflections
The daily activity as a psychiatrist, especially in the current era, leads me to constantly reflect on the causal reasons for what are defined as "disorders of mental functioning" and their interferences on the development of a balanced, linear, functional, tuned and integrated existence with the ecosystem. In simpler words, a well balanced life.
This objective appears to be possible to reach for all living beings (for their brains), but for various reasons it is still not possible to fully achieve.
 The reflections that will be made do not claim to be exhaustive or explanatory of the complexity of psychic phenomena nor to suggest universal solutions or specific therapies.
The approach is only oriented to take note of the existence of such phenomena (paradoxical), and hypothesize that perhaps these are inevitable processes, part of an evolutionary phase still in progress and that "Mother Nature", despite everything, will make her course.
This awareness, however, could help our brains to modulate the state of "psychological suffering" in the face of the numerous paradoxical and bizarre events present in the "natural" human behavioral repertoire.

PART I

1. The real history of the human brain

Reflections and questions on the evolutionary aspects and the functioning mechanisms of the most extraordinary biological structure ever known in the world

A small amount of biological material, with a gelatinous appearance and a volume of about 1200 cm^3, this is the identikit of a system with amazing vital properties combined with incredible destructive potential.
A complex mechanism whose alteration in the operating conditions can provoke extrinsic changes big enough to possibly endanger its own survival and that of the environment in which it lives.
Is it possible that the fate of the planet "Earth" and its inhabitants are in the hands of around three pounds of gelatin?

What is the brain and what is its function?

Before embarking on the discussion of those aspects of the brain that most of all arouse confusion, it is appropriate to make a brief reflection on what the brain really is and what it serves. The answer to this question is not as simple as it might appear.

Let us start by saying that any life form has a self-control apparatus, called the Nervous System.

In relation to the organism in which it is "inserted" and to the "tasks" it must perform, the nervous system can be very simple, that is made up of a few cells with few filaments (axons and dendrites) and limited connections (neural network), or on the other hand very complex.

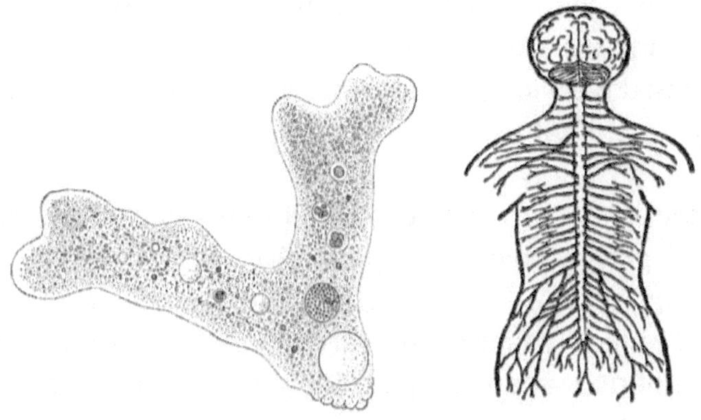

In the second case, going up on the evolutionary scale, we observe nervous systems consisting of many layers or agglomerates of cells, joined together by networks of filaments that are increasingly complex.

In the case of their simplicity or structural complexity, the nervous systems perform their task very well, which is that of "controlling the bodies" in which themselves are inserted and of which they are an integral part, allowing them to survive, reproduce and adapt as best as possible to the environmental conditions in which they live.

In other words, each nervous system represents a complex of command and control, which is an aggregate of information processing circuits, more or less complex, which is able to govern in a precise and finalized manner every single district of the body that from it depends.

In common language the central nervous system is often identified with the "brain".

In reality, from the anatomical point of view, the brain is only the most extended part of the central nervous system. Next to it there are other structures such as the cerebellum, the brainstem and the spinal cord.

In this context we will use the term "brain" to identify the whole set of the functional architecture of the central nervous system.

As for the "human" species, the brain, as an organ, has developed progressively and parallel to the organism, in an evolutionary process that, according to the available data, lasts about 2.5 million years (think carefully, 2.5 million years! An enormous period when compared to the very short life cycle of human organisms).

It means that every human being today has a family tree of 35 thousand ancestors in a direct line, assuming for each an average life of 70 years. This is true if we want to limit ourselves to "hominids", considering Homo Habilis as the oldest among the ancestors.

Following a more rigorous line, the "pre-human" preparation process can be traced back to 4-5 million years ago, with the Australopithecus genus. This is in fact, among the primates, the first known form of primate that conquered the erect station (bipedalism) and that possessed a cranial capacity similar to current anthropomorphic apes.

Normally we are led to consider the architecture and functioning of our brain as stable.

It is difficult to imagine it as an organ susceptible to further structural and functional modifications, yet it is not so.

The current structure is the result of evolution, the result of the needs and situations that, over the millennia, humans have had to progressively face. Translating our genealogy into biological terms we can say that each of us represents the result of tens of thousands of reproductions of human organisms. As a quantitative/temporal comparison term, consider that between us (today's Italians) and our respective ancestors who lived at the time of Christ's birth (during the Roman era), there are only 28 individuals. So only 28 reproductions, which also made some small differences. The present and future necessary adaptations will inevitably provoke further modifications of its structure.

Now, we find ourselves faced with a gelatinous mass, almost identical to that of other "primates" for weight, conformation and basic bio-molecular components.

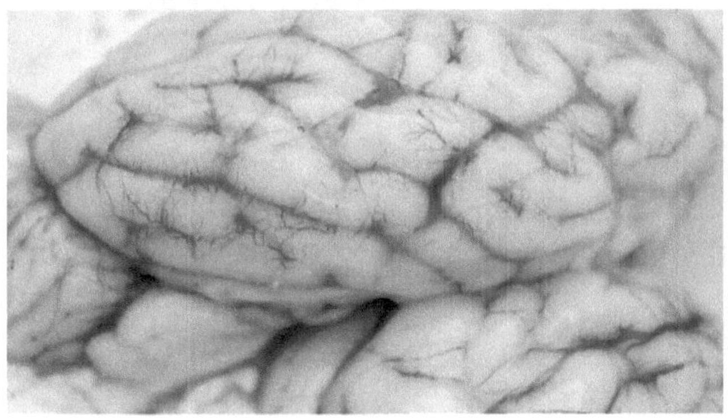

The only substantial difference consists of the development, on the outermost part of the human brain, of a layer of cells about 2 millimeters thick, which if spread over a surface would cover an area of about 1.5 square meters. That's all.

A huge "additional biological microchip" of 1.5 square meters x 2 mm thick, composed of billions of small cells closely connected to each other by millions of meters of electric microfilaments.

Does it all depend on the operation of this huge matrix?

Yes, it really seems so.

What does the brain want?

Simply to make the body in which it is inserted feel good and under its control.

In fact, its survival and well-being also depend on the correct functioning and placement of the body in the environment. An automatic and unified process that can be described very simply as the Latin sentence "mens sana in corpore sano".

Translated, the brain seeks the absence of malaise.

Examining the higher faculties of our nervous system, specifically the features that distinguish humans from the remaining living beings, it is interesting to note that they have reached an exceptional degree of complexity from only about 10,000-15,000 years ago.

Before this time, it is not inaccurate to represent Homo Sapiens as a living being much closer to other primate animals, governed mainly by instinctive automatism to defend its physical integrity and reproduction of the species.

The use of the brain as an organ that "thinks" and "communicates realistically what it thinks" seems to coincide with what we can define the beginning of history.

In the scaffolding of the body, therefore, the brain represents the seat delegated to:

- analyze and integrate all the information coming from the senses (sight, hearing, smell, touch, taste);

- organize/control the issue of targeted movements and behaviors, as well as express and clearly communicate the product of its activity (organized language).

But in addition to external stimuli coming from the sense organs, the brain, thanks also to the memory factor, can produce "activities on its own".

This is, undoubtedly, the most extraordinary faculty that in the process of evolution has increasingly refined and which has allowed homo sapiens-sapiens to reach the current goals of adaptation.

The faculties of thinking, reflecting, analyzing, imagining, planning, deducing, predicting and so on are just some of the extraordinary and peculiar activities that take place automatically in the brain of every "human" being.

Probably also in the brains of other animals, with mechanisms unknown and incomprehensible to us. But there is more. In addition to producing activity on its own, the most extraordinary thing the brain has developed is the ability to convey the contents of its activity through language.

In the flow of daily life, we do not stop to "think" how our brain is working, about what is happening in the complex network of neurons (about 100 billion), as we do not for the other organs (heart, liver, kidneys, etc.).

Regardless of our will, everything works automatically and harmoniously, consequence and expression of an incessant and complex biochemical reaction that is triggered by the fusion of two "incomplete" cells (oocyte and sperm) and proceeds automatically for the whole life span based on the genetic information contained therein.
Usually only when something does not work properly and some disturbance is detected, our brain begins to reflect on itself and on the body, that depends on it more analytically.

2. Birth and development of a successful system

The development of specific areas of the human brain (cortical areas) is directly related to the spontaneous need that the precursor of modern man, throughout hundreds of thousands of years[2], has had to sustain like shaping materials (for the construction of tools) to use it for the most disparate purposes, from the most basic ones (hunting, constructions, etc.) to the more sophisticated ones (artistic, musical, social, communication, etc.).

Let us think, for example, of the motor area (frontal lobe) and the complex network that is activated when a "brain of today" decides to screw a very small threaded screw into its seat. It is trivial for us.

However, the visual, spatial and motor coordination activity that is expressed in this simple task, especially if there are interfering factors (changes of position, inclination, brightness, etc.) is not present in any other species and does not seem easily reproducible by robotic electronic devices, or at least not with the same parameters of flexibility and adaptability that man possesses.

At the basis of a simple gesture such as that of fastening a small screw there are, in fact, unique and typical factors of the human

---

[2] The temporal dimension of evolution expressed in such high numbers deserves to deeply be considered. For the first phase, we speak of "Billions of years". It took all this time to ensure that the bio-molecular mechanisms typical of the vital reaction triggered and stabilized in the matter. Then, millions of years have served to develop its complexity and variety, with an unceasing and exponential growth. Hundreds of thousands of years, however, have served for the slow, progressive and inexorable structuring of the human brain in its current form and function.

species: first of all the biological and genetic predisposition, then learning, memory, will, motivation, logic, fantasy.
We could also think about the extraordinary brain activation that occurs when playing an instrument.
Could any other living being conceive, communicate and execute a work like those developed by Mozart, Beethoven, Verdi?
Certainly, an electronic synthesizer can reproduce it faithfully, but would it know how to conceive one? Certainly not!
Parallel to the construction of increasingly sophisticated brain circuits for motor control, which allowed man to survive better on the earth's crust, is the brain's ability to communicate through codes (sound-language and visual-writing) and reflect on itself (dialogue or internal communication).
Little by little, step by step, the complex and sophisticated structure of the brain began to produce that spontaneous activity, on its own, which we now call speculative ability or abstract thought or even reasoning, aimed at understanding the why of things and attributing meanings.

A constant evolution of the system

Reflections on its origins, thinking about something after death, the birth of social ethics, although not directly genetically transmissible because of "cultural" concepts, are all activities that can take place thanks to the growth in the brain of further circuits and connections. Then, a masterful integration with the pre-existing ones (mainly vegetative reflexes and motor automatisms) until the brain evolved towards the structure we know today.

Obviously, as already mentioned, it is to be expected that this process will not stop at the current stage. The functional needs, current, and future, will in fact condition their progressive modification.

If we think about it, in comparison between more evolved living species the biological structure and functioning of the various organs and systems are almost identical (heart, lungs, kidneys, liver, muscles, bones, blood).

Even for the brain, the basic biological matter is similar. What changes, however, is its functional organization. Could a chimpanzee today ever read, understand and comment on the ink marks printed on this sheet of paper? What about the skills connected to the upstream processing mechanisms or the editorial and typographical aspects.

The answer is undoubtedly negative, although the overall volume of the chimpanzee's brain is only slightly less, 98%, than that of man and its genetic makeup identical. Instead, for any human who knows the interpretative code of these signs (the idiom) it is a trivial thing that requires minimal effort. Yet the simple reading operation triggers extraordinary bio-electrochemical processes: the stimulation of the retina, the transfer of impulses to the decoding brain centers (visual area of the brain) on electrical wires (the optic nerve), the visual and spatial representation of graphic signs, the attribution of meaning by comparison with what was previously learned (memory).

And then again: the coordinated and sequential association of multiple meanings, the development of a concept, the association of multiple concepts, the attribution of an overall meaning in relation to the already known, the possible emotional reaction to the final meaning.

All this in an infinitesimal time and with the unlimited flexibility of interpretation, through an activity that the human brain is predisposed to optimize in an amazing way within a few years of birth. Using computer language, we could say that there is a predisposition for the spontaneous development of various operating systems and the installation of numerous programs or files that serve the organism to survive, reproduce and adapt to the environment. All according to well-defined biological rules.

The cornerstone of life

For the high value that is attributed to its functioning, the brain can be said to correspond to the essence of life itself. We can, in fact, easily accept the potential replacement of any other function of the body through natural or artificial, internal or external devices (heart, lungs, kidneys, limbs) and maintain their personal identity and free will, but we would hardly accept the idea of sustaining the upper brain functions with artificial devices (if this is possible).

We think, in this regard, of the aspects and consequences related to the state of brain death. Social rules, in fact, especially in the western world, have evolved to the point of protecting the presence of brain vitality to the extreme.

Even if the matter is the subject of debate, it can reasonably be said that to an individual whose body is completely paralyzed, who have an absolute need for cardiac and respiratory assistance, who must be nourished and purified from artificial parenteral waste and who has lost all executive nervous functions (speaking, moving), however, the dignity of "living" must be attributed on condition that those functions that support the "state of consciousness" are preserved in his brain. Difficult, pitiful, suffering, but still life.

So even a limited, but specific, autonomous functioning of the brain is sufficient to define "an existence". Vice versa, when brain functioning is absent (brain death or absent electrical activity) despite the presence of satisfactory and autonomous functioning of all the other organs, it is conventionally established that it cannot attribute the dignity of "life".

We consider it the centerpiece of life and this is why we respect it, consider it sacred, and are afraid to touch it. Instinctively we accept interventions or drugs for the body more than those for the brain. Yet mental disorder or improper brain function can potentially create more internal and external damage than any other disease in other organs.

A great narcissist, with little self-criticism

Thanks to the extraordinary level of sophistication achieved, it was obvious for the brain to feel "at the center of the Universe", consequently behaving as the master/guardian of the environment and attributing itself to the role of the main protagonist in the representation of Life in the terrestrial ecosystem.
On the contrary, it was much less obvious to take responsibility for one's mistakes. The brain is not only the creator of one's greatness but also of one's limits.
From any perspective you want to see the problem, the pivot of the question lies in the incredible complexity of the so-called "mental processes". Among all these, we observe some that we could define as "primary", deriving from the decoding of specific areas of the chromosomes and therefore genetically transmitted.
These are circuits that make up the automatic operating programs, those that activate and support the essential instincts for the development of life itself and that we find in each of the animal species of our planet. These processing mechanisms remain fundamentally unchanged throughout our life and they do not vary significantly from individual to individual (or even from species to species). This allows an easy interpretation from the outside, guaranteeing mutual understanding between living beings in those contexts where misunderstanding would result in a threat to survival.

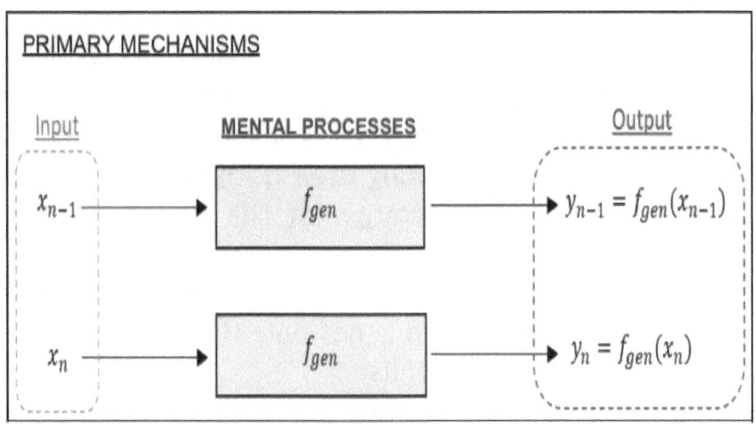

Mental processes are constant throughout the life of the individual and depend only on the input, following a genetically transmitted mechanism.

Then, there are some circuits that we could define as "secondary", not contained in the genome and therefore not inherited at birth.

They are formed through experience, perhaps from intrauterine life, and it is the operational programs that serve the development of the life, of the relationships and the search for the best possible adaptation.

They are placed mostly in the cortex (the additional biological microchip) and, given their secondary nature, they are strongly conditioned by the primary circuits and by the baggage of experiences matured by the individual and by the way in which the latter are stored in the memory.

In this case, the response functions to different stimuli are recursively updated while considering the new relations between input and output, deducted (voluntary or involuntary) by the individual.

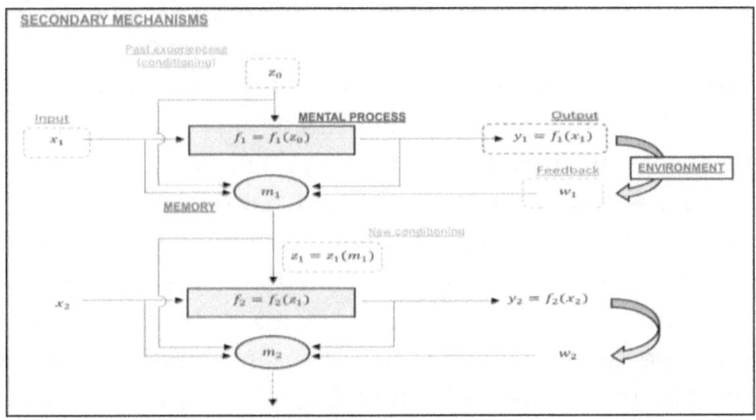

Mental processes are affected by past experiences of the individual

The resulting "conditioning" depends essentially on the arbitrary correlation that the brain establishes between the n-stress and the n-1 stimuli preceding it, both in input and output. And it is precisely from the close and incessant functioning and reciprocal conditioning between these mechanisms that the peculiar traits of every human being emerge: dignity, pride, self-esteem, sense of self, personality, character, ethics, morality, up to the concepts of tradition, culture, social structure, shared by the various ethnic groups.
Very often these factors, as we shall see, rather than facilitate seem rather to complicate the life of relationship and human existence.

During its existential activity, in fact, almost no brain believes it can function improperly, attributing to the other "systems" any interaction anomalies. What derives from this is the widespread perception of being in the right to prevail over others and in the duty to condition its functioning.

The reasons behind the natural misinterpretation of others' behavior lie in the ways, which are anything but linear, with which our brain processes external stimuli and, based on its own experience, produces an output. Differently from what happens for the "primary" processes linked to survival, whose interpretation is, as already said, immediate for almost all living species, the functions of response to secondary stresses present personal components that are difficult, if not impossible, to decode. This ultimately produces the following interaction "bias":

- Condition of misunderstanding.
Everyone interprets other's behavior (see output) based on his own response function, thus arriving at an incorrect evaluation of the motivations (see input) behind such attitudes.

- Attribution of anomalies in other people's mental processes.
In a completely specular way, everyone is led to waiting for a response to specific solicitations in line with his own mental transfer function, irremediably clashing with outputs other than those expected. Hence the instinct to prevaricate above.

- External causal attribution.
If the only correct mode of operation is that carried out by one's system, the individual confines the causes of error solely

to the boundary conditions. The result is an incessant tendency to seek external causes, to find justifications, to blame others.

3. Critical Reflection

The exceptional functioning of the brain has allowed man to send probes to the borders of the solar system, to observe, manipulate and use the smallest components of matter, to modify the genetic structure of life, to move from one point of the earth to another in a very short time with ingenious mechanical means, to assemble the matter to build colossal works.
Once these amazing properties have been verified, it is legitimate to wonder why the brain is not able to prevent the dysfunctions that afflict itself and the body in which it is inserted as effectively, preventing a truly functional adaptation in the surrounding environment.

What is expected?

According to a rational-mechanistic logic, we would expect an operation characterized by greater regularity and reliability
From any process of evolution, both biological and technological, what is expected is always an improvement in the functions and final performance. Any pre-existing "defects" or "inconveniences" should theoretically be eliminated and, in any case, put in a position to not interfere in a crucial way with the essential functioning of the system.
If we stop to reflect on the dynamics of evolution of other "biological forms", we rarely observe strongly ineffective "schemes" to survive evolution and negatively influence the subsequent adaptation.

If this were to occur, the survival of the species would be at risk.

The same applies to technological systems.
To give an example, in the automotive field we have always invested in research and development of technologies able to increase the performances of the engines, with the aim of introducing solutions that are more efficient each time and to minimize the transfer of eventual defects from the current generation to the next.

Although sometimes this is technologically impossible, the philosophy of improvement at the base of each new project efficiently prevents the propagation of critical errors and avoids the involuntary creation of new fragility within the system.
Any design direction outside this logic, on the other hand, would be incapable of evolving in a functional way and would end up being abandoned by the automaker.

The technological metaphor, of course, is very clear and does not claim to worthily represent the human variables at stake.
However, it highlights the apparent paradox behind the evolution of the mental faculties of the human being. While responding in general to the same logics that are characteristic of "winning" systems, the mechanism for improving the intellectual abilities of our species was not limited to enhancing the dominant characteristics and confining those that were ineffective as in all other systems (living and otherwise), but on the contrary, it has introduced significant elements of fragility that are completely new, looking backward on the evolutionary scale.

What is it found?

The process of evolution that has characterized the brain of the human species does not seem to have produced the complete "uninstallation" of some pre-existing files, with the result that they continue to operate and, often, to interfere with the proper functioning of the "operating systems".
In fact, it is quite evident that, unlike other living species, in the human species exceptional adaptive potentials coexist alongside frankly self-injurious and potentially destructive behaviors.
No other species deliberately, persistently and scientifically engage in activities harmful to itself.

Furthermore, based on a simple principle of equivalence it is also legitimate to assume that in the activity of evaluation and control carried out by equal systems (the functioning brains of all humans), given certain variables, identical answers must necessarily emerge.
And instead answers do not seem so obvious and predictable.

The extraterrestrial ethologist

At this point the doubts begin and some questions.
But let's imagine that it is a third subject, not specifically involved in existential human dynamics.

We hypothesize, in fact, that an "alien" scientist stops to analyze the planet earth from an ethological point of view.
Obviously in a cosmic time frame, of at least hundreds of thousands of years.
The earthly one, conventional for our brains, would in fact be too limited.

Let's try to parameterize the birth and the evolution of the planet into the 24 hours of the day.

With the following scheme, we will have:

0 1 2 3 4 **5** 6 7 8 9 10 11 12 13 14 15 16 17 18 19 **20** 21 22 **23----24**

4.5 Billions of years of Earth in relation to the 24 hours

00:00 time zero: formation of the planet
<u>05:00</u> birth of life and development of primordial biological molecules; **first chains of DNA**
<u>20:00</u> appearance of the first clamps.
23:00 appearance of dinosaurs
23:40 disappearance of dinosaurs
23:55 appearance of hominids
23:59:59': *cerebral volume doubling of hominids - Homo Sapiens*
23:59:59&999 ms. **Industrial** revolution.

Returning to our Alien, he, like a researcher dealing with a sample to be examined, would observe with his microscope the characteristics of the earth's surface and the variety of living corpuscles that grow on it. Focusing on the latter, he would try to study its characteristics and classify them according to specific parameters (number, size, life cycles, etc.). After not too long observing our Alien would notice that among the various "living" species there is one that, over time, has distinguished itself from the others in many aspects.

First of all for its physical characteristics; roughly cylindrical-shaped beings, composed of multicellular aggregates, with four extensions, two of which are in contact with the ground, the other two attached and hanging on both sides and a spherical protuberance in the upper part equipped with various orifices, mostly symmetrical. Then he would be struck by their dynamism and their vitality, so much so that he would have no difficulty in noticing its spread over the entire earth's surface and the ability to reach and colonize every part of it.

Furthermore, he would be struck by the aptitude of these individuals in manipulating and shaping the material and using it.

It should be noted that, although their average body mass is not among the greatest, using instruments they are able to contrast and even overwhelm and tame other living beings of much larger size and higher strength belonging to other species.

Also using particular instruments, they are able, then, to move faster than the other living beings from one point to another of the "terrestrial sphere" on which they live, managing to cross both the air and water components or to perforate them, when necessary, even the most solid and compact part.

The Alien, perhaps, would notice in the behavior of these cylindrical beings that, by a taxonomic convention, it will be called "human", apparently inexplicable characteristics in the peculiar modalities and purposes of the use of instruments derived from matter.
Which we will shortly examine.

4. A new perspective of time

To better understand the discussion related to the duration of evolution that has affected the terrestrial living matter, I think it is useful to use a little imagination and to consider the dimension of time from another point of view, detaching it from the perception we are used to as humans.
Let's try to analyze the time variable from a cosmic point of view.
To the question, are there, in the cosmos, the day and the night, or the succession of the light-dark cycle that gives rise to the division of the hours, days, weeks, months, years, centuries, etc.
The answer is no.
These parameters were elaborated by the human brain when it became aware of this periodic rhythm and expanded the knowledge and skills to measure it.
This conquest proved to be useful to mark our existence and place us in the history of the terrestrial globe (a tiny particle in the immense universe).
But if we consider this variable from a cosmic perspective it is nothing but the consequence of the automatic rotation of the planet around its own axis, whose surface is heated and illuminated alternately by the star "Sun".
In relation to the duration of the average life cycle of humans, a period of one hundred or one thousand years constitutes an enormous segment of time, which the brain struggles to represent itself clearly as a whole.
But if we consider the phenomenon for what it is, or rotations around its own axis of a spherical body, our hundred or one

thousand years correspond to 36,500 or 365,000 rotations. Cosmic inertia, but a significant period for our brain.

Now let's imagine that the Alien ethologist observes the terrestrial sphere in its rotating action and decides to date the vital history of the terrestrial corpuscles based on the turns of the sphere itself around its own axis.

He would note that during the last 3,650,000 turns (corresponding to about 10,000 years in the distribution of time as currently conceived), within the "human" species some aggregations of individuals have begun to use particular tools to stop the "vitality" of other individuals, not only of different species but also of their species of belonging, risking in such actions to lose their vitality.

And this is not due to an immediate or apparent satisfaction of the instinct to feed or to survive.

For other species too, overpowering behaviors would have been observed but these would appear mostly directed towards elements of different species and in a very limited number, the ones strictly necessary for feeding for survival.
Without the use of special tools, based only on one's strength and physical ability.
And, not insignificantly, they would almost never be intentionally lethal towards exponents of the same species.
Then the Alien would ask questions.
Do less widespread and "advanced" species suffer from the same disorders as "humans"?
It would seem not.
Does their life cycle run smoothly?
It would seem so.
So, why are paradoxical behaviors that seem to challenge the harmonious adaptation to the environment only in the reproductive and vital cycle of the "human" species?
The Aliens probably would not know how to explain the phenomenon.
We as "humans", directly involved, may be able to.

A big dilemma

The problem can be framed in the perspective of the evolution and history of human "thought", that is, of what were the considerations and explanations that man, or rather his brain, has elaborated when he became aware of his existence.
The real question, therefore, could be: why did living matter develop this faculty?

The attempt to answer this question, due to the characteristics of the brain, has found development through various channels: philosophical, religious, ethical, biological, etc., each with its own logic.

In fact, reflecting on oneself, starting from the last ten millennia (only 3,650,000 turns of the earth around its own axis), seems to have become an irrepressible need for the brain.

Even if the precise beginning of a "meta-psychic human thought" is rather nuanced, with the historical data available we find that some figures of thinkers distant in time, such as Socrates, Plato, Aristotle (just to stay at our latitudes), or Confucius, Buddha, and before that the priests of the Mesopotamian, Egyptian, Mayan civilizations or the biblical figures of Abraham, Moses, were credited for having played an important role in providing plausible explanations about the meaning of life.

To them, during time and in parallel with what we call the development of civilization, many other figures have succeeded each other in ever-increasing numbers, mainly religious and philosophical schools, more recently also of a scientific type.

In many respects, however, so far no one has found a universal consensus or has formulated completely comprehensive hypotheses.

Perhaps due to the inherent limitations of the human brain's activity itself in this phase of its evolution process? Or perhaps because the essence of life is truly mysterious, inaccessible to any form of reasoning, even the most sophisticated, and should be accepted as is, simply by "trust"?

When was the beginning of rationality?

One thing, however, is certain, the biological structure of the brain has begun to produce its marvelous speculative work only recently (at 23:59 pm and 990 ms of the cosmic day).
Now, if we look at the adaptive evolution that has affected the structures of the various organs of the human body over the millennia, we note that the changes in functioning have been minimal. The heart pumped and continued to pump blood into the vessels in the same way. The liver continues to metabolize nutrients using the same chemical processes. The lungs exchange oxygen and carbon dioxide with the same mechanism.
And so on and so forth, for all the other devices and organs.
All, in any case, seem to be subject to the automatisms of the chemical-physical laws of matter, in this biological case shared by all the living. Therefore, similar physiological basic processes always achieve the same results. For the heart contraction and thrust of the blood fluid; for liver degradation and chemical transformation of materials; for the lungs exchange of gaseous molecules.
For the brain, on the other hand, the speech seems completely different. If it is true that the chemical-physical processes of basic functioning have remained substantially identical and common to the nervous systems of all living species, even those of flies (the excitability of the membranes of neurons and their property of transmitting and propagating electrical impulses) the product of this activity for today's human brains is not identical to that which occurred in the brains of 10,000 years ago, even with the same structure and chemical composition.

Especially for what happens in the operation of the outermost part, the additional one: the cortex.

The pulses continue to be generated and propagated in the same way, the electrochemical components are the same.

What has changed and continues to change is the qualitative and quantitative "motivation" in the genesis of certain impulses: those that support the so-called higher functions, mental activity proper.

In fact, the nerve cells of our 100,000-year-old ancestors functioned in the same way as ours.

What has radically changed is the result of the bio-electrochemical activation that occurs in the processing of stimuli and the neuroendocrine consequences that trigger (emotions, feelings, moods).

Take, for example, the ways of interpreting some natural phenomena.

The nearest star, the Sun, could be (and indeed has been) interpreted as a divine entity.

The modest terrestrial satellite, the Moon, a mysterious and influential element in life cycles.

The eclipse phenomenon, as a work of gods and a sign of catastrophes.

A natural electrical discharge such as lightning as a hostile activity of unknown agents.

The other animals of the environment with special powers.

The perception and evaluation of these elements, made by those brains, in that specific evolutionary period (only 3,650,000 revs ago) led to interpretations and consequently behaviors: fears, emotions, rituals, behaviors, and relationships with others and environment.

Today we would call them "primitive", absurd.

Yet they were produced by the same basic nerve structures that we find in the cranium of today's humans.

Therefore, the same electrochemical impulses, in the same biological tissue, although generated by the same stimuli, by the mere fact of being modulated and addressed in different cerebral microcircuits produce completely different consequences in the whole organism.

In fact, the belief of the "Sun" as a god caused typical emotional states, reasoning and behavior. Completely different from considering it as a star that generates heat and light. And so on for all the various phenomena.

While the heart, the liver, the lungs ... continue to function in the same way and produce the same result in the wonderful human machine.

5. An extreme experiment

To get an idea of the composition and specific functionality of the human brain, let's try to reflect on the consequences of a hypothetical extreme experiment.
Let us imagine the separation of two monozygotic twins (two perfectly identical individuals from the point of view of DNA) at birth: the first entrusted to the exclusive care of an adult, sound-minded "deaf-mute" nurse, who, while living in a condition voluntary social isolation, is able to use adequate nutritional sources for themselves and the child, is able to guarantee the right protection from environmental dangers and from infections, is also able to offer adequate parental care and be a valid guide in exploration activities of the surrounding world.
Condition, as mentioned, purely experimental, but potentially concretized in some areas of the planet.
The second, instead, is bred in a context typical of Western culture.

Imagine a comparison between the two brothers at the age of 6/7 years, when the basic processes of brain development are almost complete.
Can we hypothesize a difference in the development of the two individuals?
Probably you would not notice any difference from the point of view of somatic growth: the hearts, the lungs, the limbs, would be identical, as well as there would be no differences in evacuative functions.

The volume of the skull and the weight of the brain would also be the same.

But let us ask ourselves: would they be equal in brain functioning? The obvious answer is no.

The first lacked many of the stimuli necessary for stimulating the development of the brain in the direction that supports the typical functioning that we currently know. Above all, an effective form of verbal communication (remember that the nurse was deaf-mute) would have been lacking, essential for the growth and development of the complex neural networks that are at the base of the higher functions (analysis, memory, imagination, etc.) or, at least, of how we know them.

The hypothesis, however, offers us the starting point for reflections.

Based on the neurophysiological knowledge we can certainly say that, in the brains of the twins, the bio-electrochemical characteristics of nerve impulses and the basic level of functioning of the neuronal circuits of the various areas are identical.

However, we can no doubt exclude that the brother's brain raised in partial isolation with the deaf-mute nurse may have developed some of the superior psychic faculties typical of those who live in a social context, even minimally, complex or even primitive: ethics, modesty, the solidarity, empathy, envy, competition.

Furthermore, could we hypothesize a sufficient recovery of its functional "deficit", should it fit into a typical social context? The latter is a question whose answer is not easy to imagine.

However, the example can help us better understand the essence of how the human brain works.

If left to its natural development we could assume that the brain of the first brother is comparable, perhaps, to that of a specimen of the human species of about 20 / 25,000 years ago. Lacking an effective form of communication, lacking the knowledge and skills necessary to fully exploit environmental resources, devoid of those superior intellectual abilities that allow us to be what we are today. But with a basic structure that can potentially acquire them all, if exposed to the right stimuli and forced to interact with other similar ones.

And this does nothing but support, even more, the extraordinary complexity and grandeur of the biological matrix that aggregates and shapes itself, in the development of the human body, as an organ of command and control.

PART II

6. Paradoxes and contradictions

A big dreamer

Today's brain is certainly able to imagine and outline a system of life and perfect adaptation.
We could say utopian.
It is a natural goal that he wants, perhaps, more than anything else. And with the correct means available, could theoretically achieve.
Unfortunately, it is limited only to theorizing it.
This happens because the higher mental processes that support this reasoning, even though they are very sophisticated and logical, paradoxically are rather weak compared to those evoked by the daily "challenges" for adaptation.
In fact, if we analyze the complexity of social norms, both written and oral, both political and of a religious nature (codes, laws, traditions) that serve to govern the coexistence between individuals in the various human societies, we cannot but agree that most of them are sharable and useful.
Their scrupulous observance could allow a course of life much less complicated than that which occurs.
In everyday reality, however, human decisions and actions still seem to be strongly influenced by instincts and therefore we are confronted with great contradictions.
A great logic does not always correspond to an equally practical activity.

Instinctive systems

To try to better understand the true essence of the functioning of the brain and its apparent oddities, in this phase of its evolution, we will try to reason by paradoxes and to highlight some of the most obvious contradictions that we often observe in activities and interactions between humans.

But before going into the discussion it is necessary to mention, albeit briefly, the role and importance of some mechanisms of operation and adaptation intrinsic to living matter, including man: instinctive systems.

It is well known that all life forms tend, in an automatic way, to survive and adapt themselves to the environment in which they live.
All this is made possible by biological mechanisms transmitted genetically which, depending on the living species, have been perfected over the millennia, and that, although imperceptibly, continue to change. And they will continue to do so as long as life exists.
According to some researchers, there are three of these instinctive systems, or rather, "programs" of life.

The <u>first program</u> concerns individual survival (commonly called survival instinct).

The behaviors that arise from this program lead us to search for food, face dangerous or threatening situations through aggression, defense or flight behaviors, push us to seek or create a haven, to defend it and protect the surrounding territory.

Today the behaviors aimed at satisfying this program are carried out through the search for a job, earning money, building a house, shopping.

Once we went hunting to catch prey, we looked for a cave or we built a hut, we personally defended our territory and our property from the aggressors.

Although the aims remain essentially the same, there are profound differences between the possible behaviors in the past and those that can be implemented today, at least in what is called Western civilization.

And it is precisely in this aspect that many of the existential problems and the basis for paradoxes reside.

Indeed, today's behaviors are no longer free or arbitrary but subject to precise rules.

If the choice or construction of the shelter was once an individual faculty, based essentially on one's physical strength and permanence on land, nowadays this may not be sufficient, indeed in almost all cases it is not at all. It is necessary to observe the constraints of a master plan, obtain the building permit, consult the architect, employ the specialized laborers and possess the necessary monetary resources.

The same could be said of work. It can also be invented, but it must necessarily be inserted in a network, in a system of competition, not only physical but also intellectual.
For one's own defense or property, it is not enough to be physically strong or to be able to neutralize any attacker with direct actions. For this there are laws or other specially designated individuals.

The <u>second program</u>, directly linked to the first, concerns the survival of the group to which it belongs.
Based on the natural thrusts of this program, we humans are actively seeking the closeness of our fellows, although not too close. The basic principle is: "union is strength".
Living and participating in the activities of a clan certainly offers greater possibilities of defense against common aggressors. It is also easier to get help when needed.
Today all this is expressed in the forms of social life, in the constitution of urban agglomerations, in belonging to factions, groups.
Also in this case, as you can see, rules have been created that often limit or contrast with some individual "instinctive" or immediate needs.

The <u>third program</u>, also closely related to the previous ones, concerns the survival of the species.
From this comes the thrusts to mate with partners of the opposite sex and to care for the generated offspring.
In the past, even not too remote, the prerogative to fertilize the female was the prerogative of the strongest or most powerful

male of the clan, often encouraged by the seductive behavior of the female itself.

Overall, however, the female was almost always subjugated by traditions and very instinctive rituals that exalted exclusively the behavior of the male element.
Nowadays, as can be seen, the rituality of the sexual approach has changed radically and has reached high levels of sophistication, taking on, in addition to reproductive, other purposes: search for gratification, exhibitionism, to become, in many cases, also a lucrative-professional activity.
All based on respect for free will and individual orientations.
It is, therefore, appropriate to reiterate that these automatic behavioral programs are an intrinsic need of the "living matter", managed and coordinated by the nervous systems (brains) of any organism.
In mammals, and in primates they are the result of an evolutionary process, perhaps more accelerated than other species, which has lasted for millions of years and served to guarantee an adapted survival.
In primates, however, at some point there was something that caused the instinctive systems to add something more, the "higher cognitive systems".
As you can see, however, (and here the problems seem to be triggered) the achievement of the basic goals of life - surviving, reproducing, adapting - nowadays must be carried out through very sophisticated behavioral repertoires, controlled by a multiplicity of anti-instinctive patterns that the brain itself, over time, formulated and decided to adopt (the rules of social coexistence) and that strenuously the brain seeks to respect.

At this point, seeming oddities emerge, what we might call brain paradoxes.
For ease of exposition we will analyze some of them in the context of the various programs.

7. Specific cases

Individual survival program: the phenomenon of opposing roles

Justice sector

In the rules of social coexistence, more specifically in the application of those that refer to the so-called legal right, we observe a series of contrasting aspects daily.
For example, let us consider the case of a voluntary murder.
As codified in the general principles of law, we know that every individual is given the right to defend himself against accusations, so that even those accused of a murder whose responsibility is obvious can exercise this right.
In a way, he also can justify what he has done.
His motivations almost always have a certain value to himself.
But what of the institutional figure appointed to protect his rights, his defense lawyer?
What mechanisms of thought must be activated to identify oneself with the reasoning of his client, try to justify it in the eyes of the community, defend it and be able to reduce the penalty to be discounted to the minimum?
The real paradox, then, would be that if he defends well, using all his experience and using possible weaknesses of the "system", he could even arrive at an acquittal judgment.
It is legitimate to suppose that his brain will be polarized towards this goal, regardless of ethical aspects, beliefs, culture.
He will come to elaborate possible interpretations on the reasons of his client, he will find some of his initiatives

legitimate, he will exalt to his advantage the importance of some formal quibbles to reach the goal.

And which mechanism, should the same lawyer have instead been a prosecutor, would have been activated?

The same brain, in both cases, should identify itself with the situation of its client, formulate justifying theories, be convinced of them, and state them in such a way as to induce the same beliefs in other brains.

Diametrically opposed theories and convictions, however, depending on the case.

The only unifying factor of this aspect corresponds to the fact that the lawyer, in both cases, is practicing his profession, and as for all good professionals the main objective is the protection and satisfaction of the client that is addressed to him and the payment of the expected compensation.

This is, in summary, the main motivating factor, or the acquisition of a "resource" (money, prestige) from which a perception of gratification/well-being will derive.

The interesting aspect, moreover, is that if the strategy has worked it will also condition and direct future behavior.

Remaining always in the field of justice, another aspect that never ceases to arouse perplexity and conflicting emotions derive from the fact that often, in the development of the various degrees of a trial proceeding against any defendant, while applying the same codes and the same rules lead to very different, if not opposite, conclusions. Guilt/acquittal, imprisonment/freedom, long or short sentence.

How is this possible? Shouldn't there be standardization in assessments, especially on a subject that has to do with the freedom of individuals?

Obviously not, and the responsibility is not to be attributed to a predefined will.

The evaluation variability depends solely on the product of the activity of the brain circuit functioning patterns of the individuals responsible for managing the matter.

It is intuitive that in the treatment of the various cases inevitably, subjective psychic variables (memory, emotions, culture, attention and analysis capacities) intervene that can determine very different outcomes.

Fault and forgive

Another human phenomenon that is strongly connected to the sphere of justice but that originates from exquisitely ethical-religious aspects and that lends itself to interesting reflections, concerns the mental processes at the basis of guilt and forgiveness. In human culture, at all latitudes and in all civilizations, brains have developed the concept of attributing a precise responsibility - a fault - to those who commit some action, direct or indirect, harmful to other living beings or to the environment, or violating rules or codes established and accepted, in principle, as useful for the collective good. Consider that a first, rough, formulation of rules useful for the coexistence of humans can be traced back to just 3,700 years ago (the famous code of Hammurabi). From the anthropological point of view, it is nothing more than a primitive step in the natural process of amplification of the functioning of the human brain, which in that phase of its incessant development realized that perhaps it was better to exploit a sort of collective and equal psychological deterrence for all (fear of a physical/biological punishment imposed by some authority in violation of a rule) instead of constantly living in a state of threat or alarm for possible harmful actions deriving from stronger individuals.
The strategy seems to have worked!
Today legislative activity is enormous. If we think about it carefully, every single human action is subject to regulation, written or verbal, ethical or religious, cultural or routine. All of them processed by the brain! It is probably one of the main factors underlying the human development achieved so far. But

as with many other brain factors, it still suffers from some instinctive conditioning. Even today we still have a strong desire to see someone who harms us punished. Even if we are sincerely asked to lose. The brain of the victim or offender ardently desires only one thing: that the culprit "pay".
That unpleasant psycho-physical state called "frustration" seems to subside only if it is perceived that the culprit, in turn, receives mental or physical suffering, both through accepted and regulated conventional procedures (compensation, imprisonment, bodily injury, in some cases death) or through direct personal actions (revenge, an eye for an eye).

Then the question that arises is: "because, despite his logical ability to understand that the damage is now done ..., the crime was committed ..., the incident happened ..., and to focus on behaviors aimed at recovering the damage suffered, does the brain "wish to perceive" that the culprit pays even if he has asked for forgiveness, is repented, has admitted his responsibilities and is sincerely willing to change? ".
It is difficult to give a logical explanation using the rationality of the brain.
There must be something else.

Avoidable waste of energy?

Further discussing the issue of justice and its fundamental role in the regulation of human coexistence, another aspect lends itself to the reasoning that, in some ways, could be considered extreme.
In my opinion, however, it is worthy of reflection.
As already mentioned, the so-called civilized countries, most of Western culture, have evolved to enact laws and regulations that safeguard individual freedom and protect the rights of all.
If we think about it, the laws that govern us and that we must respect are not so bad, at least in theory. In stabilized democratic systems in general they are the result of analytical processes, perhaps slow, of results that may not be universally shared due to the different political roles, but certainly are not detrimental to fundamental human rights.
At the same time, other systems for regulating cohabitation have also developed: religions.
These, if you will, have even greater persuasive power, as they relate to more emotional components of the brain: ethics, morals, generosity, solidarity, respect for life.
They also have effective systems of deterrence (sin, eternal punishment, penance, rituality, belonging to a group).

In an overall view, then:
- on the one hand, we assume that all the norms and laws, as well as all the religious precepts that we must observe, are good and their respect would be very useful for peaceful coexistence.

- on the other hand, however, we observe the existence of a portentous organizational system that has the task of monitoring and enforcing the laws, punishing those who transgress them.

About the second aspect, we cannot fail to note that the human components and the commitment devoted to these tasks have enormous proportions.
The police corps, which with their capillary action play the role of deterrence and repression.
The judicial systems, with the impressive ranks of judges and lawyers, who have the task of assessing guilt or innocence.
The prison systems, which would aim to inflict the "deserved" punishment and attempt to rehabilitate the offenders.
All these components require considerable resources and are a significant component in the state budgets. At least the most advanced ones.

Now, if the laws are just and the human brains have evolved to the point of developing satisfactory systems of coexistence and can understand the usefulness of the laws themselves (given that precisely these brains have developed them), for what reason should police bodies, judges, lawyers, and prisons exist? At least in such proportions?
At this point it is legitimate to ask ourselves: "Would not the simple observance of the rules by all would make the necessity of these components and the enormous investments connected to them fail?".
In theory, yes.
Unfortunately, reality offers us a very different scenario.

Despite good laws and excellent spiritual precepts, human brains continue to transgress and, consequently, to commit enormous resources to prevent, judge, punish or redeem.

Paradoxically, this occurs above all in countries with the highest technological and civil development, and incrementally even in the so-called developing countries.

As if to say that the social and democratic growth of a human community must necessarily be accompanied by the complexity of judicial systems and not vice versa, as would be logical to expect from more developed brains.

In this regard, we could also ask ourselves: "but in the more 'primitive' human systems or those considered to be less 'democratic', is the level of judicial activity smaller or greater than that recorded in the most advanced human communities?"

In other words, the social norms that regulate the life, for example, of the Indians of the Amazon or of the inhabitants of African forests or of communities that for their history and geographical position are "released" from the bureaucratic controls typical of nation-states, produce a good social justice? ... or are there cases of judicial errors in which innocents are convicted or guilty declared innocent?

Furthermore, are the set of rules that govern the social life of theocratic states or states founded on religious traditions, such as those of the Islamic world, perhaps less effective in guaranteeing an orderly coexistence and produce many more judicial errors than other systems?

Probably not.

The result in terms of effectiveness is perhaps the same in all contexts.

In all cases, there will be just judgments and sentences, less just, and glaring errors.

Probably, from a statistical point of view, no less than what occurs in complex systems such as those of developed countries.

One could object by saying that the less complexity of small communities facilitates coexistence.

In part, it may be true, but we must always consider what are the human motivations to transgress or not to norms.

In reality, a significant start in the process of reducing resources for justice purposes is already underway in some human societies (Scandinavian countries) while in others it has never reached excessive levels (Polynesian islands, isolated tribes).

Reflection

The birth and development of "Law" can be considered a wonderful product of the human brain during its evolution. A product that has significantly influenced the development and progress of mankind.

However, we cannot ignore the fact that this product has a very young history compared to that of the organ that elaborated it: just over 2,000 years for humans living in the western part of the globe (the Mediterranean and Greco-Roman civilizations) and about 2,500 for those living in the eastern part (Chinese and Japanese civilizations), compared to the millions of years of brain biology.

The history of modern man teaches us that the birth and improvement of the law, in a truly democratic sense and respectful of fundamental human rights, has had a very troubled path, almost always with enormous human sacrifices. Without reaching, however, homogeneous levels of "sophistication" among the various human groups.

In fact, two thousand years have not yet been enough to ensure that the existence of the inhabitants of the planet is universally managed in the same way.

What is observed, however, and which represents the "paradoxical" aspect is the fact that complex societies have a sophisticated system of law, in need of a huge organization, and huge resources for its management (as highlighted above).

While less advanced human societies have simpler management systems for collective existence, one could say primordial, but equally functional to the needs of the communities themselves.

Commercial sector

Many concepts and rules have been developed and affirmed in the context of human economic systems.
One of the deepest seated is the right to private property or the possession of material and monetary assets.
Therefore, let us consider the case of buying and selling an asset as important as a house.
The seller, obviously, based on his personal and detailed reasoning, will try to get the maximum profit from the operation.
Because of his deep convictions, he will try to exalt the positive characteristics of the building as much as possible and minimize its possible defects.
He will, therefore, assume a certain mental attitude and try to condition the brain of his interlocutor, a potential buyer.
When, in turn, the same person will find himself in the role of buyer, "the same brain" will develop a series of diametrically opposed concepts.
The convictions of the current situation may even drive away from the precedents as if they had never circulated in the same brain-organ.
In one or another guise, the prospect of maximizing the business becomes predominant over all other aspects.
Through the conclusion of a good business, in fact, the achievement of a very important instinctive purpose is guaranteed: the triggering in one's own body of a feeling of pleasant well-being deriving from the attainment of a purpose considered useful and coveted. Let's also call it satisfaction, gratification, or fulfillment.

It simply corresponds to a state, not only mental, that most humans want, research and, of course, try to replicate as much as possible.

Evaluation of physical or material damage.

Is the glass half-full or half-empty? Everyone draws water to their mill.

When emotionally involved, the perspective and the assessment of damage changes a lot depending on one's position.

If we must compensate, then issue resources, we tend to justify, minimize it.

"What do you want it to be, it's just a small wound?"

A blunt trauma or a fracture? "If you heal, they heal very well".

If we are to be compensated, the scenario becomes the opposite.

The small wound gets complicated, the blunt trauma or fracture will surely have a weakening outcome.

Car damage? It can be interpreted as a simple dent easy to adjust or as serious damage to the supporting structure.

Reflection

It is evident that in the reality of the many situations that resemble the cases mentioned above it can only be so, that is that the brain in any situation always aims to obtain the maximum for itself and for the body that it must govern.

Therefore, a concept is highlighted: the influence of the role assumed in the evaluation of things (subjectivity). And it could not be otherwise!

In the absence of this attitude an aspect that was fundamental for the development of humans would be lost: the motivation to do.

The apparent contradiction in the attribution of a certain value (positive/negative, useful/useless, mild/severe) to the same arguments, or situations, on the part of the brain, when it is involved in an evaluation process, is probably to be considered a phenomenon of high operational sophistication, functional to the achievement of the best possible adaptation.
It cannot be easily repressed or suppressed.
It seems, in principle, to "resist" the impetus of the norms or ethical values developed subsequently and which are also widely shared.
Often the contingent reality requires more but the brain instinctively tries to adapt these principles to its own purposes assumed in the role.

Economics/Economic competition/Competitive struggle

The complex social structure of the so-called advanced civilizations works, as we have seen, based on the rules that have established themselves during human history.
Spontaneous rules, born from the need to coexist as peacefully as possible and to progress in the various fields of knowledge and knowledge.
Since the primordial phases of their evolutionary history, humans have demonstrated competitive behaviors: to conquer a territory, explore others, adapt to the habitat by interacting with it.
All aim, as always, at surviving, adapting, and reproducing.

The current rules of coexistence, however, no longer allow the clear majority of people to exercise those basic functions of life in an autonomous or self-sufficient manner, as instincts would encourage them to do.
Let us, for example, continue to examine the need for the "shelter" in which to rest, mate and raise offspring (e.g. the house).
As already mentioned, this can no longer be built arbitrarily in the place where it is decided that it is the most useful for itself, perhaps challenging and driving away from a previous inhabitant.
Today the choice and the acquisition of the "refuge" must take place according to precise rules.
Whether we like it or not, we must adhere to the regulatory plan, to the environmental constraints, to the construction rules, to the criteria suggested by authorized experts, etc.

Since most of today's humans do not have the technical means or the ability to build it on their own, the desired and necessary "refuge" must simply buy it.

To achieve this, however, it must achieve a "monetary purchasing power" through other channels. Among these the most common is the exercise of work.

Today, man no longer must fight physically and directly against others to conquer the living space, venture into unknown places to capture prey or have a territory to cultivate.

Through the mechanisms of learning, cultural tradition and civil education, competition has moved to a different, more intellectual level.

The basic motivation, however, remains unchanged: that of providing the best possible adaptation for itself.

And then the brain is forced to work and decide based on the conditioning of two forces:

environmental factors (limits, prohibitions, obligations, rules) and innate instinctive drives.

What is the strongest or most conditioning aspect? Who will prevail in this inner conflict?

It is very difficult to accurately predict.

In human evolution, those that seem to prevail, in any context and in any activity, have been, and still are, behaviors aimed at achieving set goals. Any individual is constantly "motivated" to achieve something.

Generally, these are objectives that are strongly correlated with the acquisition of a condition deemed useful for adaptation. In more recent human history the objectives seem to be predominantly those connected to the attainment of a "power", very often patrimonial/monetary but also of social "status". But are we sure that the achievement of the objectives set by an individual or a group does not cause unjustified or disproportionate damage to other individuals?

Obviously, the answer is negative. And then we can witness numerous and continuous paradoxes. For example, we are always fascinated when we propose the personal history of an individual who, thanks to his talent and tenacity, reaches important positions, in any sector, from finance to business or management roles in complex organizations, both public and private. We undoubtedly remain fascinated in learning, as "external" observers, the exploits of the character in question, as traditionally such stories are proposed.

Our brain considers it a model to imitate or draw inspiration from. However, almost never are we led to reflect on the number of possible "victims" that the deeds of that protagonist have provoked. In any competition, someone's success inevitably leads to the defeat of others. Consider, for example, the field of finance (very topical at this historical moment).

The ability of a financial operator to take advantage of the opportunities that arise and earn considerable money profits instinctively arouses a certain admiration (today perhaps a little less).

Never, however, do we push ourselves to consider the possibility that his work may have been a significant element in the suffering of other individuals or those who have lost part or all the resources invested, those damaged by the bankruptcy of the company involved.

Conversely, if the first piece of news we analyze concerns the aspects of suffering or the dramas resulting from a certain financial transaction (crack, bankruptcy, wild speculation), the immediate evaluation of our brain will almost certainly be one of repulsion, disdain, criticism.

Even in this case, the same situation can cause diametrically opposite reactions in the same brain. It depends only on the moment, the context or the perspective in which the situation is learned and evaluated.

Reflection

If there is one thing that has allowed man to reach the current condition of development (like it or not) that is his competitive nature. Need, as is known, sharpens the talent. And of necessity to be satisfied there have been and still many there will be. It is unthinkable that the contradictions resulting from this impulse cease to exist in a short time or to condition human behaviors, only because we take note of them. Human intelligence, however, could (and should) limit its most serious side effects, tending towards the creation of a human society in which the competitive push for resources is more balanced and modulated.

War/Deterrence/Violence

As already mentioned in the introduction, man, since he has reached the awareness of his "being" and has developed superior intellectual abilities to communicate, regulate social relations and exploit his own genius (e.g. the faculties of the brain), has understood that in order to better adapt to the surrounding environment, exploiting its resources, it had to compete with other similar ones, individuals belonging to different social groups but with the same aims.
Human conflict arises from the conflict of interest for the attainment of vital goals at various levels: between individuals, between families, between clans, between tribes, between complex societies such as cities or states, between nations, between races and ethnic groups.
At a broader social level the need to compete has influenced the very composition of the social structure, making some individuals dedicate themselves full-time to the use of force and specialize in defensive or offensive tasks: military bodies.
If this necessity, at the beginning of human civilization, could somehow be understood and justified for its survival purpose, the current state of "cerebral" evolution appears completely disproportionate and, from an ergonomic point of view, inadequate.
The application that the human brain has dedicated to the development of destructive tools and devices, especially in recent decades, has been exceptional for the goals achieved: nuclear devices, missiles, planes, satellites, submarines, ships, lasers, etc.
Think, for example, of the use of submarines.

Is it not absurd that humans are forced to spend long periods of their lives in narrow spaces, hundreds of meters away underwater, with all the risks this entails, for the sole purpose of deterrence or threat to other humans?

The same applies to the gigantic amount of resources committed to designing, implementing and operating other instruments of war.

Is armed deterrence implemented by some peoples towards others necessary, with the enormous amount of resources and investments that follow?

Let us ask ourselves, therefore, if in practical terms all this activity brings real advantages to human well-being.

Reflection

If all this happened and was done, it may have been due to a contingent and intrinsic logic of the brain, at least at the beginning of human history.

But come to think of it, from a rational point of view, a question emerges spontaneously: does the total energy nowadays used in this field fit into an optimal relationship in the face of the consequent benefits?

Geopolitical strategists would say that it is a necessary evil, useful in preventing potentially more damaging conflict conditions for humanity.

Furthermore, weapons are mechanical objects that require design, experimentation, industrial production. In simple words: they represent an enormous job opportunity for many humans and a source of profit for an entrepreneurial elite.

Which always brings us back to the famous basic instincts of human life.

Food and food devotion

Eating, of course, is a primary requirement of life and, therefore, constitutes the goal of many human behaviors.
The methods of acquiring food have changed profoundly, over the millennia.
If the supply of food, both in terms of quantity and quality, once depended almost exclusively on the physical strength of everyone, nowadays as far as the western world is concerned, the supply depends on other factors.
An obvious result is that, for many humans, paradoxically, the state of health can deteriorate due to too much food.
Diabetes type 2 or essential hypertension, are just some of the possible medical conditions deriving from a "conscious" excess of nutrition.
Not to mention obesity.
Often the control of the quantity of food that an individual must introduce into his system, to ensure a correct balance of vital functions, seems to escape rational logic.
Let's think about celebratory banquets for celebrations or holidays. The amount of food that you are forced to intake requires, in these cases, a considerable effort and an excessively long time.
Rejecting a certain dish or a culinary specialty is almost impossible, despite already being full.
Often the goal is no longer to "taste" the dish or use it merely for nutritional purposes.
In these cases, self-justifying reasoning mechanisms are triggered: I wonder if I will have it again, ... for once it does not

hurt, ... it does not happen every day, ... I will burn it with exercise, ... I can't offend the guest, and so on.

The problem is compounded by the fact that the socio-cultural set-up and the commercial pressures mean that the "celebratory" occasions follow one another with ever greater intensity.

Another trend, then, is to attribute to food an exaggerated value of "self-therapy", so that we find ourselves eating, even alone or outside the usual rhythms, to appease the states of emotional tension resulting from everyday life.

Since the "gratification of the palate" or "of the throat" works very well as a temporary calming, the tendency to reuse it is obvious and automatic.

There is no doubt that the ease of access to food is a positive evolutionary factor that the human brain has achieved by its high level of sophistication and the various promoter factors that are derived from it (economic-industrial, scientific).

To get the food we need today, we are not required to stray too far from our shelter and we do not run the enormous risks associated with hunting for prey, hard work in the fields or the uncertainty of the harvest. It is enough to acquire, in some way, the right monetary resources and the needs are more than satisfied.

However, the availability and significance attributed to food can also compromise its balanced use.

It is a source of great pleasure; sensory gratification, socializing, etc., but at the same time it can also generate enormous frustrations; pressures to maintain certain body standards, often trigger bizarre, obsessive behaviors, or pathologies (bulimia, anorexia, binge eating).

Eating, or eating food in a balanced way to live better seems a very difficult thing for human brains to achieve.
The real paradox, therefore, consists in the fact that for the humans of today, at least for those settled in the so-called evolved geographical areas, we have arrived at a reversal of the processes: "living to eat" and not "eating to live", using food also (or above all) for purposes other than simply nutritious ones. This means, very often, first we eat (in excess) and then we run to burn.
In previous evolutionary phases, instead, one ran first (to capture the prey) and then ate.
But the dimension of the paradox assumes enormous proportions if one takes into consideration the quantity of energy dissipated in one of the most widespread existential schemes: working (expenditure of energies)-> acquiring monetary resources to eat (in excess)-> forcing oneself to strenuous physical exercises (for caloric burn) often depriving themselves of monetary resources acquired with another previous psychophysical effort/effort.
If we consider it from an economic point of view, considering a cost-benefit ratio, and therefore of a rational brain process, the entire cycle can be considered decidedly unproductive.

Reflection
One reason is, all the dynamics of nutrition are still subject to the instinctive conditionings inscribed in the brain circuits, therefore genetically established.

For example, the satiety reflex is activated approximately 15/20 minutes after the stomach bag has been filled. This is because "our ancestor" was not always sure of success when he went hunting or gathering. Consequently, faced with the availability of nourishment, the command system (the brain) has adopted mechanisms to capture as much as possible, in excess for immediate needs, but vital for any subsequent deficiencies. The combination of this instinct, still present, with the enormous availability of food and the socio-cultural drive to consumption, determines a hard drive to counteract, even for the most sophisticated part of our brain. The hope of a balance lies in the intervention of evolutionary processes of adaptation that will inevitably happen, but that we humans today probably will not have the pleasure of seeing.

Group survival program: Spectacular, Identification, Fashion

Another operating condition present in the human brain is the tendency to identify itself as models or stereotypes, whether they are natural or spontaneous or artificial or created by others. Owning an object or looking like, in behaviors and clothing, models, seems to be an indispensable requirement in human groups to achieve the alleged condition of well-being or adaptation.

Conformity or homologation, in many cases, can also facilitate coexistence and interpersonal relationships. Problems arise when the identification process is total, resistant to criticism or irreversible. If the reference model is threatened, collapses or suffers a defeat, then the rest of the homologated/identified ones are dragged along with it.

We observe, for example, what happens in sports cheering. If in the competition our team should lose, at best we feel, for a few moments or a few hours, a little depressed. At worst, we dump all our hatred or overt aggression and violence on those who put us in this condition.

And vice versa, in case of success the situation is diametrically opposed. In practice, that the team with which we identify lose or win to us there has not been removed or added to anything physical, no threat is caused to our heritage or to our loved ones and no advantage comes from it.

And yet, despite the conscious basic absurdity, very intense emotions or certain behaviors are unleashed because of success or failure.

Reflection
The instinct to belong to a group is still able to generate and sustain very strong identification mechanisms.
When threatened, even symbolically, as in the case of the defeat of the chosen team, automatic evaluation processes are triggered in the brain that induces behaviors of obvious hostility towards the rival, or its symbols, since it constitutes the cause of our frustration.
The purpose of these behaviors, probably, is to "exhaust" the effect of the substances produced by the stress condition. However, the outcome of the evaluation process also depends on many other factors and on the degree of self-control exercised by the brain itself.
The paradoxical aspect is that in human brains rational processes easily give way to the biological force of the mechanisms that are at the basis of instinctive processes, still present.
Species survival program: Falling in love, Infatuation, and its consequences.

It is a commonplace saying that "love is madness".
This definition is not entirely improper.
The amorous emotion is wonderful, sublime, able to generate behavioral programs and actions out of the ordinary within the brain in which it is produced.
We think of romanticism, poetic and artistic inspiration or, in more practical aspects, the push "to do" to achieve an objective related to the loving or erotic sphere.
But what is this strength based on?
Essentially this strength is based on the brain mechanisms inscribed in the survival and conservation program of the species, which are sustained by the production of hormones and neurotransmitters that activate specific areas of the brain itself and of the body.
These produce the pleasant body state typical of falling in love and eroticism, which in most cases translates into an unstoppable push.
Could he ever do without it?
The instinctive component of this program is strongly conditioned and exploited by the activity of brain circuits of more recent construction, the so-called higher ones.
It is these, for example, that prevents the act of sexual mating in a direct way from being explicit, based on physical presence only (for the male) and external availability/attractiveness (for the female).

As far as the human species is concerned, the dynamics of the search for a "preferential sexual partner" with which to produce and raise offspring have evolved over time, as:
- more useful (concentrating on one person reduces wasted time and energy)
- less risky (there is no need to physically fight with other competitors for the same partner)
- more functional to the care of the offspring (the efforts are more concentrated and aimed at the protection and education of the children, which will grow better and will then be more constrained and, perhaps, useful for future support).
Over time these behaviors have even been incorporated into real rules of social coexistence or have received reinforcement from their mystical-religious representation as if they had been dictated by entities external to humans.
Let us think only of some of the aspects enunciated in the ten commandments of the Judeo-Christian religion. "Do not desire the woman of others".
The application of this rule takes on extraordinary value for the orderly development of society.
His observance greatly limits male conflict for the search for the sexual partner and its consequences on the physical plane.
His association with the other principle "Do not fornicate" then completes the picture and protects the monogamous relationship, one of the major goals in the evolution of the human species.
Linked to this we find, then, "Honor the Father and the Mother", which means creating a policy for old age. Everything seems logical and consequential, well-articulated, acceptable.

Yet everyday life subjects us to an infinite variety of behaviors that deviate from such well-structured concepts, which even a part of the brain has learned, shares and constantly tries to affirm in contrast to the more instinctive forces.

It is no coincidence that some areas of the body if targeted by appropriate stimuli produce pleasant global neuro-sensations (sexual, visual, gustatory, olfactory, tactile).
They are functional and basic to the achievement of primary (instinctive), fundamental and automatic goals for survival.
The current human brain cleverly exploits the great "intrinsic biological force" and the automatisms that derive from it.
Always and solely to achieve the same adaptation goals.
The erogenous sexual zones are cleverly used, under the direct control of the brain, to give rise to the variegated behaviors aimed at a fundamental vital process: reproduction.
There is no doubt that the appropriate stimulations of these areas (especially genitals or their neighbors) produce, always under the coordinated and integrated control of the brain, perceived bodily states and recorded as highly rewarding.
And like all pleasant things, they are the object of active research.
Unlike other living species, however, an impromptu "replica" based on physical prevalence is not allowed for human animals.
Thanks to its sophisticated cerebral and social evolution, at least in the so-called developed communities, the implementation of sexually rewarding behaviors, both for reproductive and pleasure-only purposes, must be carried out according to determined rules of respect for individual freedom, modesty, conventions, of laws.

The paradoxical aspects that pertain to this area all stem from the contrast between instinctive and instinctual force aimed at the pursuit of pleasure and the constraint of having to observe rules (family, social, legal, ethical, religious, etc.).

It is very easy, and very widespread, to squander or divert personal, economic and non-economic resources towards goals that must do with amorous-sexual-erotic fulfillment.
In this case, how many times is it observed that the man "x", of a certain age but endowed with economic availability, has joined the women "y" attractive but not very wealthy? ... Often even to reverse roles!
It is a widespread phenomenon, which at a superficial evaluation generates feelings of hilarity, of ridicule, to the point of qualifying the whole as inappropriate or illogical.
But for those directly involved there are no suitable arguments to break up the "logic" behind the choice.
For both there is the fulfillment of an instinctive need (in this case the affective/sexual need for one and that of survival for the other. And vice versa).

What would the sex industry be based on, if not the existence and strength of this vital instinct?
A session of sex mercenary, with partners with physical characteristics considered "model" can be paid, by those who can afford it, with high figures.
These, from a rational perspective, if used in another way, would be adequate to allow a family to survive for a month.
The brain that decides to buy such emotions is perfectly aware of it.

Yet he decides otherwise!

Examples of this kind, relating to the affective-erotic-sexual context, are in the thousands.

We think, to stay on the subject, of the behavioral frivolities of people in love.

Do not pay attention to gifts, travel miles to reach the beloved, utter phrases that one would never dream of saying, write poems.

It is also very easy to work in actions that transcend normal courtesy in favor of significant people related to the partner to be conquered (brothers, parents, friends).

Any request is answered; although considered absurd, exaggerated, untimely.

But faced with the potential threat of a loss or impairment of affective-erotic-sexual satisfaction, the human brain elaborates clearly incongruous strategies and produces decidedly uneconomical actions.

The phenomenon of voluntary abortion, or, rather, Voluntary Interruption of Pregnancy, is one of the human behavioral aspects that have recently been affirmed in the repertoire of recognized rights.

In the debate that still exists on the legitimacy or otherwise of such a practice there are theories and principles for and against.

All follow their own logic and motivate their supporters. Often only due to the "obligation" of belonging to a social group.

Obviously, the theories and the concepts in favor or against are the result of the elaboration of brains, which are conditioned by the relative working mechanisms developed with the experience and are oriented, as always, to guarantee the best adaptation to the respective bodies.

If we analyze the contents of the opposing theses we observe that:

- those in favor attribute to the woman the right to decide whether to continue an unwanted or unsustainable pregnancy;
- those against the focus on the fact that every form of life, even in an embryonic state, must be protected.

From a right point of view, there are probably plausible arguments in both theses, so much so that abortion is lawfully practiced by all national health services and is also allowed to refrain for professionals who do not want to practice it. Both positions are protected by precise rules of civil law.

The aspect that however surprises and highlights the paradox deriving from the sophisticated activity of the brain consists in the fact that while recognizing that the vital biological reaction of fertilization is the expression of the instinct of conservation of the species, therefore useful for survival. Even if humans cannot govern it as they claim to do, and could do.

Heterologous sexual relations can lead to the fertilization of oocytes and the development of embryos/fetuses and therefore new people.

However, we are constantly witnessing the fact that human brains activate the process of coupling-fertilization in an instinctive, often simplistic and sometimes unconscious manner, to which they are "forced" to remedy with abortion.

Expressed in terms of a biological economy, this phenomenon is truly paradoxical.

There is no single species in nature that "repents", so to speak, a reproductive act and deliberately activates itself to stop it if it has been successful.

It is not in the logic of biology.

Instead the human brain has devised sophisticated concepts to admit and practice anti-biological action.

About the product of fertilization, some brains have even gone so far as to define the temporal and structural limit between "pre-human" or "human" entities.

That is the difference between the aggregate of cells " arbitrarily expendable" without any problem (because of the small number) or a more numerous cell aggregate that is therefore "worthy" of greater legal protection.

It is true that a state of pregnancy can derive from non-consensual sex, out of a classic family project, or the result of an uncontrolled sexual-erotic practice, and it is easy or useful, and technically possible, to remedy these conditions with abortion.

Due to its great power and functional sophistication, one would expect that the human brain, consistently with the natural biological principles (which also underlie its operation), should be able to avoid the triggering of an unintended reproductive reaction and aimed at the conservation of the species.

And instead we see how easily numerous brains are conditioned to look for sexual mating behaviors not aimed at reproduction.

Obviously, these aspects are more present in the so-called developed human communities, where they are supported and reinforced by an extensive socio-cultural sexual solicitation for hedonistic and recreational purposes, both spontaneous and commercial.

If we look at less technologically developed human communities we note that the practice of abortion is non-existent. Simply because sexuality is managed spontaneously and its reproductive consequences are accepted as a natural phenomenon, not interruptible with artificial expedients.

Reflection

The preservation instinct of the species, of any species (including the animal man), is based on the great strength of the sexual drive and its behavioral repertoires.

Despite its great sophistication, the human brain, in its current level of development, does not yet seem able to modulate this driving force or limit its consequences if not finalized. Even in the brains belonging to so-called advanced human communities.

From this arises the enormous paradox, which makes him admit and implement an anti-biological practice to remedy his obvious self-control deficit.

Translated into simpler terms: the human brain seems to like the erotic-sexual solicitation not aimed at reproduction.

So more and more "play and get gratification" with the reproductive organs.

Unfortunately, and here is the paradox, with a lack of awareness of the extreme ease of release of seminal fluid (very little is enough to determine an ejaculation), its enormous biological-vital potential and the wide availability of fertile "soils" (less awe in female sexual behaviors and greater performance).

From sophisticated brains like the current ones, one would, therefore, expect a less "unnatural" management of the phenomenon than that adopted so far.

It is undeniable that from the simple encounter between the two-incomplete spermatozoon-oocyte cells, a biological reaction is immediately triggered that contains the complete expression of life.

Justifying at any cost, based on sociological concepts, the need or opportunity to suppress a vital biological reaction, arguing over which era divides the reaction into a true-life form from one not considered as such, seems to be among the pseudo-philosophical loopholes subordinated to practical convenience. Exactly like other opportunistic paradoxes.

But a truly scientific and rational brain cannot fail to admit that the "biological life reaction" begins exactly in the act of conception.

8. Modern society: stress and derived syndromes

Statistical data on mood disorders, especially depression, indicate that between 15 and 30 people out of a hundred suffer (the figures vary according to the sources) and that their number is constantly increasing. These disorders affect all age groups, young people, adults and the elderly, even if the female sex, overall, is affected slightly more.
Not to mention anxiety spectrum disorders. Also in this case, we are witnessing an incessant increase in cases of panic attacks, phobias, generalized anxiety crises.
What was this increase due to?
No doubt in part due to the improvement of knowledge in the specific field and to an appropriate scientific framework of mental disorders once considered on the margins of medicine.
But next to the greater diagnostic refinement we can undoubtedly assert the importance of stress today.
Speaking in the context of stress would open a huge chapter.
Let us limit ourselves, therefore, only to considering the essential aspects and to recalling some concepts expressed previously regarding instinctive systems.
First, let's start by saying that stress (which in English means equivalent to a "state of tension") is a condition of activation of the organism when it is called upon to do something more than the state of rest.
So, it would be better to talk about "stress reaction" caused by exposure to a stimulus (stressor). This, as we will see, can be external (traffic, noise, physical constraint, threat) or even come from within (a negative forecast, an unpleasant memory). This last aspect seems to be typical of the human species.

In general, we can say that a stress reaction is activated whenever there is a need to satisfy one of the instinctive systems based on life.

When the automatic systems of evaluation of the brain (consciously or not) revise their necessity, they trigger a biochemical reaction that serves to increase the global power and capacity of the organism to face and overcome the need of the moment. Generally, the needs to be addressed are aimed at: defending oneself, procuring food, mating for reproduction, caring for offspring, maintaining social bonds. As already mentioned, these are always the basic prerogatives of "living matter", including man. When the actions, both automatic and consciously processed, implemented because of the stress reaction are effective and the need is satisfied by the brain, then the reaction is defused by the brain itself and the organism re-enters a state of functioning basal (engines idling again). In this case the stress was positive, it helped us to overcome the need (we passed the exam, we found the solution, we removed an enemy, we defended ourselves or our loved ones, we found a partner). Problems arise when our actions, for reasons dependent or independent of us, are not able to overcome the need and achieve the goal. Since the brain acknowledges but still believes it necessary to do something, the biochemical reaction of stress remains activated for a long time. This, in summary, creates a sort of functional depletion of resources (the motor and the connected circuits overheat and overtime no longer work properly). Over time, the damage is also caused by the structures.

At this point we have entered the field of pathology, both psychic and physical. Since this brief introduction, we can find valid reasons that justify the increase in disorders resulting from stress, and establish, consequently, from a general economic perspective of human biological resources, that these are real operating paradoxes.

Based on what has been extensively discussed above and of the specific cases illustrated, it should therefore not be surprising that the brain function of the "representatives of the human species" (e.g. all of us), especially in this phase of its evolution, can lead to self-produced dysfunctions. Let's see how and why.

First, we must remember some already established concepts:

- All life forms tend to the best possible adaptation.

- Adaptation is often equivalent to gratification in life's goals.

- The achievement of the fundamental goals of life in the context of human interactions is now implemented through ever more numerous and sophisticated behavioral and communication strategies.

- Not everyone can or is able to implement them in the same way.

- Wanting but not being able to implement/achieve generates frustration, which is equivalent to stress.

- As a result, impaired functioning and possible self-produced disease.

Some examples?

One of the broader sources concerns the world of work for subsistence and of family members.

In this context, we find a whole range of possible conditions sufficient to trigger negative stress reactions.

The competition to be judged better, to earn more, not to be exploited, is not always successful, for various reasons: the superiority of others, the contingencies of the moment, the lack of means, etc.

And it is quite difficult for a brain to accept or easily rationalize such defeats.

At least not immediately.

If we believe that the other has been undeservedly awarded, or that we deserve more for what we do (whether it really is or is just a mistake of (sub) evaluation), the stress reaction can easily be triggered because the brain considers of not having reached a condition of better adaptation possible for himself.

But examples of stressful events can be drawn from all human behavioral environments in which there is a minimum of competition.

A typical predisposing condition is described in Appendix 1. Do we want to change it?

9. Criminal organization and mind weakness

Among the various human aggregations there are some that procure (enormous) resources to live and adapt with activities that exploit the weaknesses of the human brain in an excellent way.
Let's consider the so-called drugs. We all agree in defining them as harmful. Yet their consumption does nothing but enrich individuals who would never dream of using them, such as managers and operators of criminal organizations.
Despite the enormous media coverage of the damages, the penal and administrative consequences deriving from the use of illicit psychoactive substances, many human brains are activated and do their utmost in every way to procure and use them.
The real paradox is that everyone, to varying degrees, is aware of the damage and the legal consequences. However, this does not seem to be a deterrent sufficient to limit its diffusion and use.

The brain itself, it seems, can manage to construct a whole series of appetitive behaviors, employing considerable resources and resources. And just as many resources and strategies must be employed to avoid being forced to abandon this use. In the context of a strenuous struggle between brains trying to counteract their use and brains that try in every way to persevere, with the only result of enriching production and marketing managers.

But not only, we think of all the elements and organizations that deal with identifying, combating or suppressing the phenomenon.
How many humans, time and economic resources are invested, wasted or uselessly used simply because the brain cannot say no to the use of substances that it clearly recognizes to be harmful.

But the discussion could also be extended to other areas of dependency. The so-called legal ones: alcohol and cigarette smoke.
Also in this case, there is a real paradox.
There is great, clear evidence of damage related to the use of these substances, with all the social and economic consequences that derive from it. Yet brains insist on consuming alcohol and smoking cigarettes.
There are brains that work hard, spending significant amounts of resources, to dissuade and cure. At the same time, there are brains that do their utmost, directly or indirectly, to support or increase their consumption.

From any point of view, we want to consider it, all the brains, in various ways involved, seem to have an interest and draw personal advantages from it. All except those of consumers. It is paradoxical but it is so.

PART III

10. Paradoxes "in pills"

Axiom of the prophet

Thanks to its level of functional sophistication and the development that it has currently achieved in the technological and humanistic field, as well as to the effects of globalization in the communication that it has itself invented, the human brain is able to be able to design a planetary model of peaceful coexistence.
It would be useful, and worthy of the intelligence they presume to have, that the set of functioning brains could do it to live it during their lives, not for future ones.

A real draws trouble

It is truly amazing to observe how the brain, in the exercise of its functions, goes very easy to get into highly stressful conflict situations.
For example:
- first engages in spasmodic research and in the conquest of affective life. Then, this often leads to highly conflicting and energetically costly break-up actions. Large amounts of energy to achieve the goal of a relationship (marriage, cohabitation) and great energy to dissolve it (separation, divorce).

Everything is strongly conditioned by having to observe the principles and rules that it itself has developed. A truly intelligent system would never be drawn into such excesses.
- Usually he persists in not giving in on matters of principle, never asking for excuses or retracting a position/point of view, even if he proves to be wrong, not convenient and often very expensive; all for the sole purpose of defending one's pride and dignity. An intelligent system would care more about what is essential.

Anthropological crime

The biggest anthropological "crime" a brain can commit?... Deceive and negatively condition, during their training, the brains that they themselves have decided to reproduce. Despite pedagogy, sociology, and psychobiology, we are confirmed with increasing evidence that many of the adaptation or antisocial disorders that develop in adulthood recognize trauma or child abuse as the predisposing factors, the brains that "command" (e.g. the adults), those who make such observations, fail to fully and universally implement what they propose. It is truly paradoxical to note how few resources or energies in practice are used to guarantee the regular development of the brains of "human puppies" in the face of the inevitable future problems that will derive from this deficiency. A possible explanation for this paradoxical phenomenon consists in the fact that the brains, in their evaluation activity, are more polarized on the current reality. The "small" problems of caring for the offspring that the children present are usually treated in a circumscribed or hasty manner. The same can be said for the problems of education and acculturation. In some respects, such an attitude is physiological. A dialogue on a par with less developed brains is almost impossible, so the stronger / bigger imposes itself on the weaker / smaller. Likewise, communication takes place in general. The result of this phenomenon is that discomfort or bad adaptation will continue to be present in future human societies. A truly intelligent system does not predispose the ground for future complications.

Blackmail strategy

A formidable example of brain activity aimed at obtaining resources or advantages (usually patrimonial or status, therefore always monetary), is constituted by the blackmailing behavior. Consequence also of the high functional sophistication of the brain, which exploits the aspects related to emotions, ambitions, ethics. Among the most frequent conditions that expose to blackmail we find those of a sexual nature, where an alleged transgression (the satisfaction of an instinct/need, made outside of orthodox schemes) becomes a weak point (due to various perspectives of affective loss, monetary, image, etc.) in which the attack of other competitors is inserted. Furthermore, the probable defense strategies implemented by the victim do nothing but aggravate the situation; unless you are willing to give up and / or lose something. But this, often, the brain refuses to do it. An intelligent system can discriminate and prevent involvement in potentially counterproductive situations ... or to deal with and manage the harmful effects.

Sublime and Golden Brains of power

In the social organizational set-up of humans there are usually a few individuals who govern the fate of many.
The choice and the role exercised by the former are functional to the operational needs of social guidance, to simplify the role of command and direction.
This is a useful process that has emerged with the social evolution of the human species and its brain. With a natural and spontaneous process, the elites have been created and affirmed: monarchies, governments, military, administrative, cultural, religious.
But let us ask ourselves: is the brain of the representatives of these elites perhaps different from that of other individuals? ... shaped by different matters and devoid of instinctual heritage? Or is it immune to altered processes? The answer, of course, is NO.
Therefore, it is essential to take these factors into consideration. The representatives of the elite, especially if they are top leaders, certainly use a lot of energy to carry out their functions, but they usually enjoy privileges and are facilitated in their tasks.
Even a man, or a woman, an important person who has conquered or been appointed by others to carry out tasks of the highest responsibility, whose only physical presence exudes an aura of power and determines a "psychological submission", well, he too is gifted of a brain organ that has developed with growth and functions according to natural biological processes.

Like all other human brains, he also aims to achieve the fundamental goals of life. Therefore, in addition to the functional integrity of the structures, much attention must be paid to the quality and reliability of the operating systems that are installed inside the brains of those who have decision-making power. An intelligent system can understand that the perfect individual does not exist, but that there is only one that fits better. Only those who do not interfere with the adaptation of their fellows among humans are worthy of respect.

It is not the weight that matters

To the question: "what is worth more, a ton of terracotta bricks or a transparent stone of 10 grams? A child or an inhabitant of tropical forests, who never had contact with the so-called western civilization, would probably give more importance to the ton of bricks, considering the mass and their possible practical use. Instead, any individual who grew up in any human society, even marginally exposed to patterns and values of cohabitation a little more evolved, would say without a doubt that the transparent stone, if identified as a diamond, has more value.
To attribute a symbolic "value" to something material was a need that was installed in the brains of humans while developing the higher faculties of analysis and introspection. But is there a true biological evolutionary reason to explain this phenomenon? Is it functional to something useful for adaptation? It would seem not, or at least not directly or clearly.

Yet how much energy human brains have been using for some millennia to research or possess inert substances to which they have conventionally attributed a certain asset value. Just think of the mines, the trade or the criminal aspects related to these substances. Where is the rationality that is considered the patrimony of a command and control body so sophisticated in its functioning mechanisms which are the human brain? If it is so easily conditioned by the charm emanating from a few grams of material, be it transparent or golden, red or green, and so on? An intelligent system would not waste enormous amounts of energy to extract tiny stones from the ground to which to assign a purely virtual importance

And so, he got stuck by himself (... the brain)

To survive, the human brain has exploited the surrounding matter by inventing and perfecting many things, up to all those things that today we produce in large quantities: means of transport, weapons, chemicals, artificial products in general.
All of this organized in the form of work, useful for guaranteeing the means of sustenance, survival and the best adaptation. Through entrepreneurial activity (there is always someone who invents and produces something) managerial and commercial (there is always someone who sells something), politics (there is always someone who uses something for a purpose).
Of all this it seems that we cannot absolutely do without (in the so-called industrial societies). Even if these activities produce a priori damages (polluting/toxic) or even death (weapons) in certain percentages, regardless of the real intentions.

But to renounce such an approach, in most human societies, would perhaps create enormous imbalances (due to the brain stresses of those affected).

We reflect on the dynamics that are triggered when we decide to close a factory or an industrial plant. It takes on a secondary role, in the immediate perspective of survival, whether this factory or plant produces weapons or dangerous chemicals or produces pollutants such as processing residues.

So, if directly involved, our brains are forced to accept and hope that any trouble or damage does not happen to us, even knowing that damage or injury will occur in safe percentages.

An intelligent system would never produce so much toxic waste that it would poison itself; he would never engage in actions where a high level of lethality is already established.

Cultural (cerebral) emancipation

The awareness of having rights, of being able to defend one's dignity, of aspiring to things that were previously impossible, etc., leads to exaggerating the individualistic concept of existence. Hence little tolerance to the defects of others or to the actions/behavior of others that we do not like. Little is thought of the real or unconscious motivations of others when they act and therefore understand the reason for their actions. Usually, we stop at the simple and immediate evidence: he offended me, he behaved badly, he didn't consider me, he ignored me, he was rude, he didn't understand me, he's not capable.

Which immediately generates a closure and the triggering of a conflict to affirm our principles and opinions.

But the other (his brain), in most cases, acts exactly like us. Then the circuit closes and is perpetuated to infinity.

Even the emancipation of women, at this stage of human evolution, is producing crisis phenomena. But it cannot be stopped in any way. Even the female brain wants to adapt to the best and develop the most appropriate strategies to do so. A truly intelligent system does not go beyond its capabilities and does not despise the limits of others.

Universal cultural / school training: advantages or disadvantages?

The educational institutions - the School - have been implemented in industrialized human societies with the express purpose of educating and educating young people so that they can build an integrated, and possibly successful, future work.

Obviously, the service is universal and extended to everyone. And everyone is given the opportunity to use them.

In the variegated human societies, it is observed that the systems and the operators of the formation study, program and work, between limits and difficulties so that their work is crowned with success. This is their mandate.

From an ideological point of view, this is tantamount to saying that all the students who begin the training course should potentially carry it out achieving the expected recognition (the title, the qualification or whatever).

Usually, and it could not be otherwise, for all individuals the objectives are initially high level (degree or qualifications for social roles of "thought").

It must be recognized, in fact, that since the beginning of the training course (primary schools) the expectations of success are present in all the protagonists in the game:
- parents, who want the best for their children;
- educators, who would like to see the fruit of their work;
- the institution itself, which draws justification for its existence and recognition from the percentage of final success to its public function.

But, just for the purposes of this book, let's try to make an extreme argument.
Let us assume that, due to a positive trend of all the variables involved (motivation of the students, skill of the educators, support of institutions and the family), the School reaches 100% it is objective (something to which it must naturally tend because we cannot certainly imagine the opposite), it must be admitted that in a short time human societies would be composed of highly educated and "theoretically" competent individuals. All adapted to managerial, administrative, planning, or conceptual roles.
Let us ask ourselves, then: would they be technically able to perform practical tasks, of a so-called "manual" level of work?

Probably not! For different reasons. It would not fall within the expectations of one's own lives, having been oriented and trained for other goals. They would never have developed the manual skills and the necessary experience because they didn't have enough time to do it. Moreover, they would hardly accept a "demoted" occupation compared to the acquired and subjectively perceived potential. In a short time, societies, absurdly, would find themselves short of basic tax rates of individuals in the production of goods and services: labor, workers, farmers, artisans, soldiers. It could be argued that many of those who have acquired a "title" should be converted to more practical roles, adapting to contingent needs. Giving up the goal that they have disciplined following. But doesn't all this taste like a paradox? In a sense, therefore, we are forced to hope that one of the fundamental institutions of human civilization will never, or at least not for a long time, reach 100% of its objectives.

What are they led to think, hope, imagine, the brains that reflect, face and are involved in various ways in this field? Expressed in these terms, it seems that one of the main products of the evolution of the human brain, the "Culture", in a broad sense, contains the premises for its failure.

But it is not so.

In my opinion, it is only theoretically a paradoxical phenomenon. Current and transitory.

Because only today, with the level of globalization achieved, brains are strongly attracted (obviously) by labor standards in which less physical effort is expected, believing vice versa, that the performance of intellectual roles is synonymous with greater success and well-being.

In fact, this is the message spread today on a planetary level, which due to its contents cannot be coveted, or inculcated, by normal brains, especially in the process of being formed.

A truly intelligent system would perhaps find a different, equally satisfying life path.

Transitory because the need to satisfy the innumerable social needs will determine the spontaneous distribution in the various roles. Eventually all the brains want to survive.

However, in a logic of coherence, in order not to be at the same time creators and victims of an evolutionary paradox, where necessary the function of the educational institution should perhaps be ideologically redefined.

This should not delude the brains knowing they do it, but be realistic.

It should mainly ensure human growth and civil training when the brain is most likely to do so.

Only later, because of personal motivations and ambitions, to offer the possibility of learning and training for specific high-level intellectual purposes.

To conclude

We need an awareness of the limits of our brain and of what it can, paradoxically, cause.
A possible solution, potentially practicable immediately thanks to globalization, is to reinforce the concept of considering us all as part of a single living colony, united by a single destiny.
Reducing the competitive aspect to "ethically" tolerable levels (a concept that the human brain can understand) can minimize the level of planetary stress due to competition by giving precedence to the sense of reality and brotherhood, mutual altruism and the sharing of well-being.
If my fellow is well, he will not be pushed into aggression to survive, so I do not have to defend myself against others (legitimate demands), I can trust them and therefore live my existence in a peaceful and balanced way.
It is the right of all living beings of the human species.
All of this has the flavor of a fairy tale and in fact the concept "if each of us does three good deeds a day ...", was the topic of a film.
But if it were really realized the global result would be taken for granted.

"Of love, I want to give so much, so that there is always enough around me!"
From an unknown author

Appendix

Persistent Cognitive-Frustration Syndrome (P.C.F.S.)

There is a new, subtle, mental pathology that seems to be significantly increasing its incidence in the human population, but with higher values in the "Italian peninsula". It is a syndrome (that is a group of symptoms affecting multiple organs and functions), which according to clinical observations using a psychiatric-anthropological approach, can be defined as "Chronic or Persistent Cognitive-Frustration Syndrome" (P.C.F.S.).
Although the symptoms that characterize it are largely overlapping with those present in other well-known syndromes in psychiatry (such as dysthymia, adaptation disorder with or without anxiety/depressed mood), it differs in various aspects both in the causes that determine it and in the possibilities of treatment and its course.
The following is a brief description of its salient features starting from its clinical manifestations. In the end, it will be possible to better understand the causes and specificities relating to the Italic population.
This syndrome, which affects males and females equally, generally within the 25-55-year aged group, is mostly expressed in people with an advanced educational achievement. In other words, it seems to have a higher probability of creeping into those brains that have formed according to the principles enunciated by the fundamental institutions of an advanced society: the school and the family.

So, all those brains that, in their development process, have been motivated to invest, with great discipline and sacrifice, many of their energies in culture, in training, and in the development of a civic sense. Altogether in the very reasonable perspective of being able to achieve a better quality of life more easily, in a better society.

But, in the personal history of these subjects the actual correspondence between what was hoped for and what was found in practical life, between what was dreamed and how realized, is determined only in minimal percentage or it is not determined at all. Some basic peculiar characteristics of these potential "patients" are:

• a reasonable level of optimism
• taking care of yourself
• practicing sports or other social activities
• being inclined to respect the rules and education
• being informed, traveling, and being open to the world.

They can, rightly, be considered as "healthy individuals", without defects or predisposing structures for overt pathologies, which have developed normally.

Once established, the typical symptoms of this syndrome are numerous and vary from states of frequent depression of mood, anxiety and alarm, possible panic attacks, irritability, and poor tolerance, both mental and physical fatigue.

Expressed in this classic way, these symptoms do not give the idea of their disastrous interference with the quality of life of those affected.

They can be confused with transient reactions to contingent issues in the workplace or family. In this syndrome, in fact, depressive states are not so serious or lasting, so they hardly induce the sufferer to resort to specific treatments, be they pharmacological or not. Often, if something positive happens or happens, the mood rises and one feels optimistic.

Then, the next bad news or negative circumstance gets depressed again. And so, it goes on in an incessant swing. Hope and frustration, optimism and pessimism, trust in the future, and catastrophic vision.

This oscillating condition, moreover, in those who are biologically predisposed, can also lead to more serious neuro-psychic dysfunctions, which are more difficult to treat and resolve. The states of anxiety, alarm, and irritability present in this syndrome are not just other accessory symptoms.

They assume fundamental importance in the progressive deterioration of interpersonal relationships and ties, both affective/marital / family and socio/work. And then it happens that: the normal and legitimate "requests" of the affective partner appear absurd claims or whims. Hence misunderstandings, quarrels, and inevitable breakups. The employer or colleague is one who wants to take advantage of it, often due to mutual distrust, tendency not to cooperate fully, etc. Family and personal rhythms become frenetic. In fact, there is often the obligation, not only economically as it happens in most cases, to exploit the skills acquired with training since the title has been obtained to do so and it would be an injustice not to exploit it. So, work.

This obviously leaves little room for peaceful dialogue or understanding of everyday problems within the family. Hence the possible rift between the world of adults and that of children. If you are lucky, that the boys, on their own, understand and adapt, the seriousness of the problems is reduced. Otherwise, the emergence of the common problems of study, social life, etc. becomes a dangerous aggravating factor for the global family crisis.

With the implementation of buffer solutions with unpredictable results. Panic attacks and persistent fatigue are experienced with anxiety and take on an invalidating value, greater than their actual clinical weight. Uncertainty about one's health conditions takes over without being able to identify immediately visible causes.
In such conditions, can one ever be optimistic, sociable, carefree, or help others?
The risk is that, by entering into this spiral, one can easily be labeled as a bad companion, annoying, protesting, or disinterested individual.
And this, in addition to not helping, certainly feeds a perverse vicious circle.

Now we come to the causes and triggers of the syndrome in question, with specific reference to the human society that inhabits the Italian peninsula.

In this area of the planet, a shared ideal of collective life was sufficiently developed (among the first in the western hemisphere) just over two thousand years ago, with the Roman civilization.

Then it suffered a drastic regression, whose effects are still present.

In fact, what we hear today, and which is supported by social dynamics, is that the "country" has yet to be built, as a human social system. Or, at least, it does not yet seem to have reached the levels of other more advanced Western systems.

The reason why it was not reached is not the subject of this observation, it concerns historians.

But the psycho-anthropological consequences certainly do. Let me explain.

Can a normal brain ever be gratified that is continually exposed to contradictory stimuli concerning its life and can strongly condition its best adaptation? Certainly not.

If the social setting tells us that "we must study", that "those who sacrifice themselves have greater chances of success in life" and things of this nature, but then the reality is quite different, the brains that must work out such conflicting stimuli will have difficulty understanding or justifying their deviations.

If the media dwells on the details and describe anguished news in the slightest detail, they foist them daily by spreading raw images, often overcoming the limits of confidentiality, certainly do not induce those who observe processes of brain processing that then translate into those physical states we call "feelings of well-being".

The natural human processes of identification and projection that are triggered in response to the perception and analysis of such events certainly do not create psychic reactions of serenity.

The succession of scandalous events, of scams, of macroscopic inefficiencies, of violence, etc., surely does not generate trust in the neighbor, especially if they involve institutions, organizations, or bodies that should not do so and from which one would not expect it (health, judicial, economic-financial, political, scholastic, etc.).

The conquest of a social position or a status only thanks to recommendations or knowledge that cannot fail to create hatred and resentment.

Certainly, the brains are equipped with defensive mechanisms of compensation and rationalization, but these have biological limits in their electrochemical functioning.

And here the most vulnerable to the onset of the P.C.F.S. are the brains of a higher educational level.

Not because the less educated ones do not understand the contradictions of society, they suffer less because the less the commitment in education was, the less their previous expectations and the dreams that inspired them and supported their motivations.

Paradoxically, we can say that the greater culture and greater awareness of their past, of their potential, is the prelude to a condition of greater frustration when things do not go according to legitimate expectations.

Which in the Italian peninsula seems to involve a growing population. That of the "normal brains".

Furthermore, the sneaky aspect is that from time to time there is something that also positively stimulates these brains. But often they are illusions that do not last long, and the relapse is inevitable.

Hence the triggering of cerebral elaborations that alternately generate feelings of optimism and pessimism, trust and disappointment, serene resignation and anger.

Another element favoring the increased incidence of P.C.F.S. among the inhabitants of the Italian peninsula it derives from the acquisition of greater openness to other cultures and from the increased possibility of traveling and comparing across cultures.

And it is this last aspect that seems to be the most relevant aspect in causal terms.

Going to other countries belonging to the so-called Western culture to study or do scientific research, staying there for tourism or work, knowing their habits and rules, or simply hearing about them and seeing images of them, generates a deep frustration when comparing experiences made with the variegated reality of the Italic community.

Above all in terms of a lack of exploitation of the obvious resources available and of the creative/intellectual potential that we are convinced we possess.

Unlike what happens in other similar pathological conditions (dysthymia or adaptation disorder) that often recognize a "fairly objectified and definable" cause and have an "individual" course, in which one can have sufficient awareness and availability/possibility to resort to specific medical treatments, in the case of the P.C.F.S. we are faced with a syndrome that simultaneously affects large sections of the population (all "normal brains"), whose causes lie in phenomena that are difficult to control or change by individuals (scandals, corruption, criminality, financial-economic crises, political quarrels, etc.), difficult to treat (not being able to change the "status quo" for the better and hoping to be able to make use of it during one's existence, as happens with other more organized human communities) and difficult to avoid (we would be required to emigrate).

Therefore, psychological dynamics deriving from desiring the right and not being able to obtain it; dreaming and not being able to realize; working and not have the right reward; competing in unequal conditions; perceiving poor governance; mistrust in the systems that should guarantee the protection of health and social justice; perception of oppression or being subjected to abuses, and other macroscopic contradictions in human interaction, are able to generate, in a brain that works according to normal cognitive patterns, a series of continuous logical reflections (hence the name of "cognitive syndrome ".) Whose result cannot but be like frustration, and, in the medium to long term, to its consequences.

The gravity and the high morbidity index inherent in the P.C.F.S. and therefore the paradox, depends on the fact that:

- the causes are determined by complex phenomena of a socio-cultural nature, which cannot be easily eliminated or modified;

- simultaneously affects large sections of the population;

- is devious because it does not determine a stable and continuous condition of "deficit" and / or the use of specific treatments. A normal brain instinctively tends not to admit to being sick. He always hopes to make it on his own;

- alters behavior, deteriorating the harmonious development of human relationships, undermining the development of the future society.

In neuro-psychopathological terms, this condition is called "hopelessness" and "helplessness", which is a condition of "helplessness/hopelessness" and importantly "without the possibility of help". The worst that a normal brain must face. To remain anchored to examples related to the Italic reality we make further considerations. The social-cultural climate (the average lifestyle) that prevails in the collectivity of Italians produces new elements of "toxicity" every day that lead to the persistence and increase of the pathology P.C.F.S.

This is not to say that in other human communities they do not exist. The fact is that in the Italic reality the harmful elements often have peculiar characteristics: they come mainly from the fundamental sectors of the country's order structure; often they have the most disparate textures and unthinkable implications. Taking a cue from recent events, a practical and emblematic example is provided to understand the phenomenology of the pathology in question. The so-called "G8 public procurement inquiry". In the case in question we have brought to the fore plots of corruption, selfishness, a certain unscrupulousness in financial management, protection of corporate interests, eccentric personal habits, in some cases hardly attributable, at first sight, to the protagonists. So surprising! Whether it is completely true or false, or something in between, it does not matter. What is pernicious and a harbinger of pathology is the meaning that derives from the various scenarios that are revealed to the public opinion by the media that, obviously, try to best perform their function by offering details, plausible interpretative hypotheses, describing minutely details and situations (note that they are always brains in the practice of a profession that seek to get the most).

Learning that there are women who offer services of a sexual nature behind payments that sometimes correspond to more than a month of work by a family man or a medium pension, could easily lead to emulate this type of "profession". Why study and sacrifice having the uncertainty of finding an "honest" job, corresponding to your expectations, without recommendations? ... is it absurd to hypothesize that a normal brain, after having "learned" it, rejects such an opportunity a priori?

And then enter a conflict state? The choices are very personal and varied, but if you don't, it's hard not to fall into frustration. Knowing that there are individuals who do corporations (the various castes) to increase or protect their interests, through ideological or pseudo-cultural collusion, with the ostentation of power and wealth characterized by barely concealed vulgarity, cannot fail to induce an indignant reaction in normal brains. Except to adapt! Many others share similar examples that occur and are disseminated in the Italic social scene. From the increasingly complicated, squalid, unthinkable, and unexpected plots.
Surprising and stunning. That normal brains just can't process! But also, knowing that someone has done it or has established himself in his profession, often leads to interpretations from the possible "paranoid" contents (... who knows or how much he will have paid?) or feelings of envy. Feeling, the latter, which during a normal training process is taught not to cultivate, but then, in real life, you inevitably find yourself in the problematic condition of having to manage. Despite, or regardless, the possession of a religious belief or amoral.

To conclude, the whole question has truly paradoxical implications. This "humanity" first reclaims and equips itself to build normal brains, potentially trained to follow logical rules, and then do everything to confuse them and generate frustration and stress in them. Triggering, in this way a "struggle" for the search for the best adaptation, which, for now, especially in the "hunting territory" of the Italian peninsula does not seem to be within everyone's reach.

Physicists, Astronomers, and Cosmologists

Among humans, there is a category of people who use their brain's faculties for a truly exceptional activity, even if almost ignored by the masses. Only episodically they are called to the fore when some event or discovery diverts media attention to their work.
Then immediately we forget that they work daily, patiently, disciplined and I would humbly add, in their observation and analysis laboratories.
We talk about astronomy scholars, in the various skills: physics, chemistry, mathematics, etc.
The "cosmic" dimension of their discoveries sometimes leads them to consider them as stars, but little is thought about the stressful daily routine, almost boring, to which they dedicate themselves. Often with long periods of uncertainty about the quality of their theories and desired results.
Overall, it's not an easy thing and it's not for everyone.

However, their work, especially in the last decades of our civilization, offered fundamental explanations about life and its origins with fascinating theories and ever more detailed documentation.

But where do these theories come from?
Obviously in their sublime brains. In their gelatinous organ of command and control, with a structure like that of many other human beings.

Comparing the contents of Greek mythology, which explained the birth of the universe and of the earth, the theories formulated and accepted today seems to make us smile.

Yet the brains of the Greeks of only 2500 years ago (912,500 turns of the earth around their own axis, and so many days) were firmly convinced that Gaia had given birth to Uranus, which Kronos would then come, followed by Cosmos.

Faced with their vastness, they thought the oceans were endless.

Furthermore, only a few centuries ago, most humans believed that Gaia was at the center of the universe. Some brains that dared to propose alternatives to such deep-rooted beliefs have been peremptorily canceled.

Yet the human consortium has gone on the same, and the set of functioning brains has equally continued to believe, speak, imagine, love, hate, kill, compete, help, build, study, reflect.

Until you get to today. Increased in number and certainly better organized to exploit the resources of the environment to survive, reproduce and adapt.

But the astonishing aspect that such reflection induces to do regards the faculty of the biological matter "brain" to produce some "intrinsic reactions" (the thought) able to delineate and to represent itself of the scenarios not immediately perceptible with the organs of sense.

Theories on the structure of the universe are based on statistical calculations, in turn, produced by brains.

This is the basic logic. And it is amazing to think that matter (in this case biological) can represent itself and its components.

Even if we do not perceive it because our sensors are limited as a structure, the speculative capacity of the biological brain is able to define with reasonable certainty (obviously according to human parameters) what happens in the immense cosmic space, how it is composed and how it moves.

But where is the representation of which one is speaking?
In the biochemical processes of the sophisticated microcircuits of the human brain. Those structured in the famous biological microchip of 1.5 square meters x 2 mm thick.
And, as far as we know, only there.
It does not yet appear that the chimpanzee (the hominid closest to us) began to study the "big bang" or to wonder what the moon is.
We could also ask: but if the brains of Aristotle, Copernicus, Newton, Galileo, Einstein, etc. or contemporary scholars had not decided to reflect on the issues on which they reflected, perhaps we would not be still offering sacrifices to Gaia or Kronos or to fear the reactions of Uranus?
Or, if the supple and unpredictable events of any human existence had not taken, in their case, the directions they took, would we perhaps have a representation of the universe like the present one and in which we believe?
Furthermore, there was no one who imposed it on him. Probably it was only the fruit of a strong scientific curiosity combined with personal abilities higher than the norm and favorable, sought-after or fortuitous circumstances.

And here we can introduce some fundamental concepts:
What determines what a brain will do or think or how it will manage the life of the body in which it is inserted?

The answer is many things, between the variables of the psycho-socio-relational human life and of the environment.
 It should be assumed, however, that during evolution if the acute reflections and discoveries that made the brains of the characters mentioned had not occurred as they were, probably some other human brain would have done the same reasoning and the same observations, at different times and places, of the same objective value.

Returning to our characters, it is also useful to consider another aspect.
We are fascinated by their hypotheses and their theories. The ease and familiarity with which they speak and disseminate the results of their studies, but where do these processes come from?
Obviously from their brains, which before reaching the stage that makes them capable of organizing such forms of thought were brains that had to study, learn, motivate themselves, become curious, memorize, organize knowledge. Guided in this by other brains that in turn had the same educational process, and so on back in time.
In an unstoppable process that could have only one direction, the "forward" one, intelligently exploiting the acquired knowledge and always adding to it the other.
We think of the progress of knowledge in the field of physics, chemistry, biology, computer science, mechanics.
The set of these disciplines has taken our gaze far beyond our Galaxy, which is also immense with respect to the speck of dust represented by the planet Earth, on which we live and feel like "giants".

The brains of our astronomers have succeeded in defining the characteristics of matter, the one that makes up the whole universe.

Let's think about it for a moment. A kilo and a half of gelatin, present in some living individuals on the surface of the planet earth, can represent to itself what is the chemical composition of areas of the universe billions of kilometers away, exploiting expertly assembled devices, analyzing, deducing and inferring on the acquired data.

It's amazing!

A very small element of the universe (man) can project his gaze to the borders of the existing and to theorize (perhaps with good approximation) the real nature.

Finally, the most surprising and fascinating thing is that all this happened in about 36,500 turns of the "Earth" grain of cosmic dust around its axis.

The study of tectonics and the movements of the continents, of biology, as well as the acquisition of all the scientific knowledge that allows us to look at our planet from the outside and to study it for what it really is, is the fruit of just a few decades of speculative activity of human brains.

Today they seem obvious to us.

But let's think about the wealth of knowledge on the planet Earth deposited in the brain of Christopher Columbus, only 500 years ago. A trifle compared to what a fifth-grade student could potentially have today.

This reflection can help us to consider the extraordinary power of the human brain organ.

Even for those who are not particularly experienced, the speeches and news concerning astronomy always arouse great interest or curiosity. For those who are supported by true scientific curiosity, the knowledge concerning the universe, its origins and its evolution, determine a psychological state of "fascinating wonder", with the probable overcoming of the ideological constraints of human nature. Or rather his brain.

But, to remain anchored to the earthly reality, let us limit ourselves to appreciating and enjoying what the numerous scholars of this subject continue to propose to us.

It is difficult to break away from the current socio-cultural dimension, from the competition for adaptation that still prevails and which in many cases negatively affects human lives.

The daily struggle for survival, in the terms I tried to explain in the previous chapters, does not leave much room for abstract reflections, even if shared.

But, in my humble opinion, it is precisely here that a key to reading can be found that allows a significant leap forward towards a more peaceful planetary order.

 Probably only with a more cosmic vision of life on the part of human brains could we overcome the "animalistic" limits still present in our brains and feel that we are all part of the same living colony.

Cleverly oriented to obtain a balanced existence in all its aspects.

As far as I am concerned, I feel profound personal gratitude towards all those scholars who have directed their vital energies towards scientific research and the dissemination of knowledge.